First World War
and Army of Occupation
War Diary
France, Belgium and Germany

59 DIVISION
177 Infantry Brigade
Lincolnshire Regiment
2/4 Battalion
23 February 1917 - 31 January 1918

WO95/3023/2

The Naval & Military Press Ltd
www.nmarchive.com
Published in association with The National Archives

Published by

The Naval & Military Press Ltd

Unit 10 Ridgewood Industrial Park,

Uckfield, East Sussex,

TN22 5QE England

Tel: +44 (0) 1825 749494

www.naval-military-press.com

www.nmarchive.com

This diary has been reprinted in facsimile from the original. Any imperfections are inevitably reproduced and the quality may fall short of modern type and cartographic standards.

© Crown Copyright

Images reproduced by permission of The National Archives, London, England, 2015.

Contents

Document type	Place/Title	Date From	Date To
Heading	WO95/3023/1 2/4 Battalion Lincolnshire Regiment		
Miscellaneous	D.A.G 2nd Echelon Base	30/04/1917	30/04/1917
War Diary	Foucaucourt	06/03/1917	06/03/1917
War Diary	Left SubSector	07/03/1917	11/03/1917
War Diary	Night	12/03/1917	12/03/1917
War Diary	Southampton	23/02/1917	23/02/1917
War Diary	Le Havre	24/02/1917	24/02/1917
War Diary	Saleux	25/02/1917	25/02/1917
War Diary	Vers	26/02/1917	26/02/1917
War Diary	Fouencamps	27/02/1917	27/02/1917
War Diary	Bayonvillers	28/02/1917	05/03/1917
War Diary	Belloy	12/03/1917	21/03/1917
War Diary	Bois St Martin	22/03/1917	24/03/1917
War Diary	Belloy	25/03/1917	25/03/1917
War Diary	Le Mesnil	26/03/1917	26/03/1917
War Diary	Boucly	27/03/1917	01/04/1917
War Diary	Roisel	02/04/1917	05/04/1917
War Diary	Templeux	06/04/1917	19/04/1917
War Diary	Roisel	20/04/1917	27/04/1917
War Diary	Ruelles Woods	28/04/1917	30/04/1917
War Diary	Jeancourt	30/04/1917	05/05/1917
War Diary	Le Verguier	06/05/1917	15/05/1917
War Diary	Vraignes	16/05/1917	25/05/1917
War Diary	Equancourt	26/05/1917	28/05/1917
War Diary	Gouzeaucourt Wood	29/05/1917	07/06/1917
War Diary	Beaucamp	08/06/1917	17/06/1917
War Diary	Dessart Wood	18/06/1917	21/06/1917
War Diary	Equancourt	22/06/1917	01/07/1917
War Diary	Beaucamp	02/07/1917	05/07/1917
War Diary	Neuville	06/07/1917	09/07/1917
War Diary	Barastre	10/07/1917	31/07/1917
Miscellaneous	Operation Orders by Lieut Colonel A.P. Johnson Commdg. 2/4 Lincolnshire Regt	26/07/1917	26/07/1917
Miscellaneous			
War Diary	Barastre	01/08/1917	21/08/1917
War Diary	Millencourt	22/08/1917	30/08/1917
War Diary	Millencourt Winnezeele	31/08/1917	31/08/1917
War Diary	Winnezeele	01/09/1917	19/09/1917
War Diary	Winnezeele Watou	20/09/1917	20/09/1917
War Diary	Watou	21/09/1917	22/09/1917
War Diary	Watou Ypres	23/09/1917	23/09/1917
War Diary	Ypres	24/09/1917	29/09/1917
War Diary	Vlamertinghe Watou	30/09/1917	30/09/1917
Operation(al) Order(s)	4th Lincolnshire Regt. Operation Order No 19	14/09/1917	14/09/1917
Map			
War Diary	Watou	01/10/1917	01/10/1917
War Diary	Watou St Venant	02/10/1917	02/10/1917
War Diary	St Venant	03/10/1917	05/10/1917
War Diary	St Venant Erny St Julien	06/10/1917	06/10/1917
War Diary	Erny St Julien	07/10/1917	09/10/1917

War Diary	Erny St Julien Hestrus	10/10/1917	10/10/1917
War Diary	Hestrus Dieval	11/10/1917	11/10/1917
War Diary	Dieval Ohlain	12/10/1917	12/10/1917
War Diary	Ohlain Souchez Area Zouave Valley	13/10/1917	13/10/1917
War Diary	Souchez Area Bluebell Camp Alberta Carency Area	14/10/1917	14/10/1917
War Diary	Carency Area	15/10/1917	16/10/1917
War Diary	Carency	16/10/1917	16/10/1917
War Diary	La Coulotie	17/10/1917	21/10/1917
War Diary	La Coulotte Chateav De Ln Hail	22/10/1917	25/10/1917
War Diary	Chateau De La Haie	26/10/1917	28/10/1917
War Diary	Lievin	29/10/1917	31/10/1917
War Diary	Lievin	01/11/1917	01/11/1917
War Diary	Lens Sector	01/11/1917	12/11/1917
War Diary	Lievin	13/11/1917	13/11/1917
War Diary	Carency	14/11/1917	14/11/1917
War Diary	Laneney	14/11/1917	14/11/1917
War Diary	Gony Servin	15/11/1917	16/11/1917
War Diary	Habarcq	17/11/1917	18/11/1917
War Diary	Bailleulmont	19/11/1917	20/11/1917
War Diary	Achiet Le Petite	21/11/1917	22/11/1917
War Diary	Fins	23/11/1917	23/11/1917
War Diary	Fins (Dessart Wood)	24/11/1917	25/11/1917
War Diary	Fins	26/11/1917	26/11/1917
War Diary	Fins Trescault	27/11/1917	27/11/1917
War Diary	Trescault Flesquires	28/11/1917	28/11/1917
War Diary	Flesquires	29/11/1917	01/12/1917
War Diary	Flesquieres	02/12/1917	02/12/1917
War Diary	Bourlon Wood	02/12/1917	04/12/1917
War Diary	Flesquieres	05/12/1917	10/12/1917
War Diary	Trescault	11/12/1917	14/12/1917
War Diary	Lechelle	15/12/1917	15/12/1917
War Diary	Bertincourt	16/12/1917	16/12/1917
War Diary	Bertincourt Haurincourt	17/12/1917	17/12/1917
War Diary	Flesquires	18/12/1917	23/12/1917
War Diary	Rocquigny	24/12/1917	26/12/1917
War Diary	Maizieres	27/12/1917	31/12/1917
Miscellaneous	Report on Withdrawal of Rearguard 177th Brigade	07/12/1917	07/12/1917
War Diary	Maizieres	01/01/1918	31/01/1918
Operation(al) Order(s)	Operation Orders No. 1 By Colonel A. Hutchinson. V.D. Commanding 2/4 Bn. Lines. Regt.	22/06/1915	22/06/1915
Heading	WO95/Stray/KK		

WO95/3023/2

2/4 Battalion Wiltshire Regiment

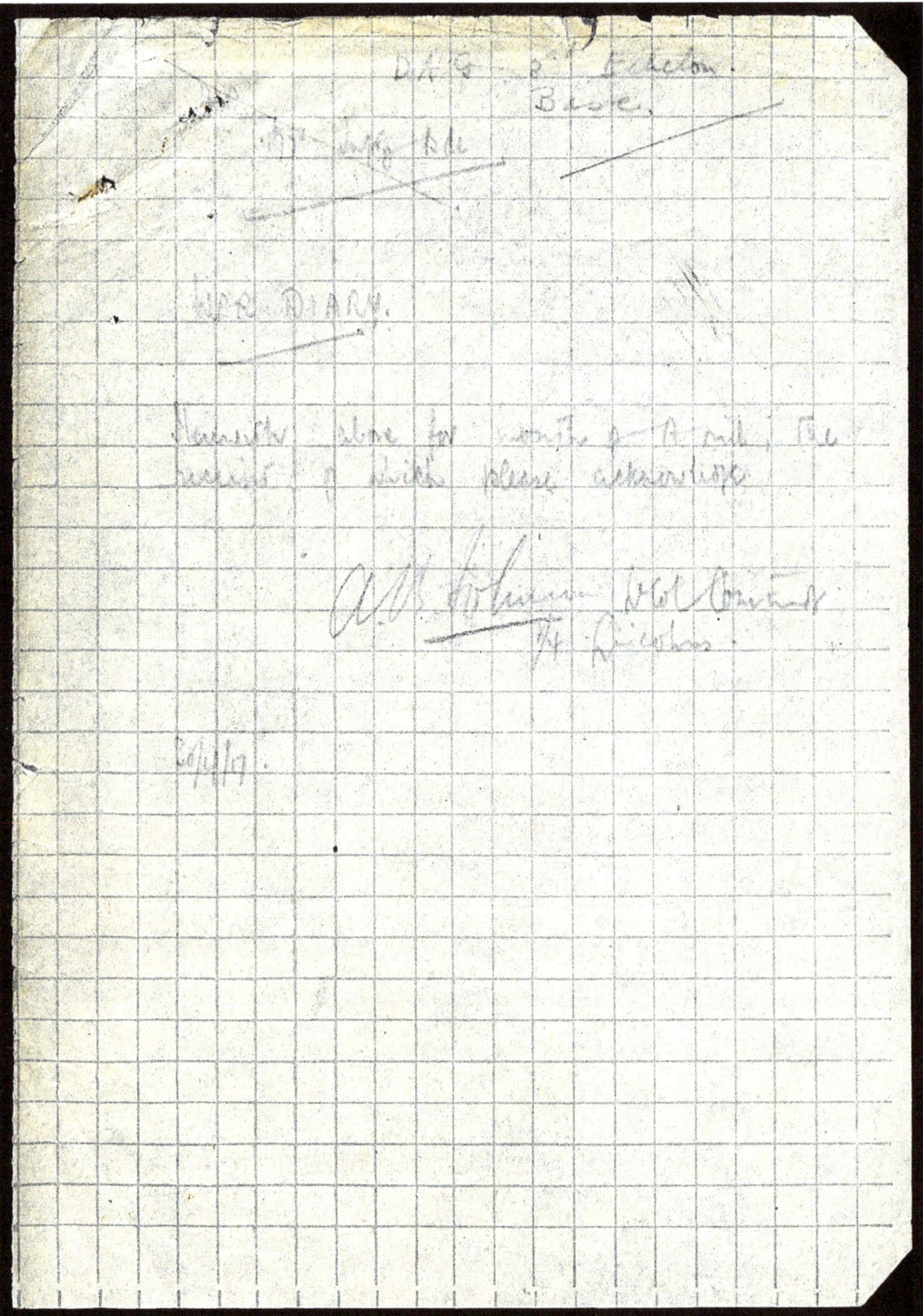

WAR DIARY
INTELLIGENCE SUMMARY

Army Form C. 2118.

SECRET

4 R'Innis'

(Erase heading not required.)

Instructions regarding War Diaries and Intelligence Summaries are contained in F.S. Regs., Part II. and the Staff Manual respectively. Title pages will be prepared in manuscript.

OC — MARCH 1917 — NOC 17

Hour, Date, Place	Summary of Events and Information	Remarks and references to Appendices
FOUCAUCOURT 6/3/17	Battalion treks on West of front line March route to ESTRÉES VILLERS CARBONNEL Road. Bn. marched 16.15 — marched up to Rancho (5 miles). Relief reported complete 22.15. Dispositions as under :- Right Coy A. Centre Coy B. Left Coy C. each two one platoon forming the composite Reserve 6. Coy as supports No casualties	AHA
LEFT SUB-SECTOR 7/3/17 10:00	Quiet day: one man wounded by a gunshot accidentally. Enemy artillery firing 5 miles north, about 17.15.00.	AHA
do 8/3/17	Quiet day: two men wounded by artillery fire — both these men O.I.S — dugouts which changed from East to North. There to a short subsequently. Wind N.W. Re BARD N° 2900 one of the casualties, died shelled 2:30 p.m. gas shells on front on left.	AHA
do 9/3/17	Quiet day; HR shelled 2:30 p.m. Gas shells on front in Wind changing to S.W. & weather warmer.	AHA
do 10/3/17	Considerable more activity the enemy in Artillery & Trench Mortars. and retaliation by our artillery. Wind South & thawing fast. Trenches again becoming bad.	AHA
do 11/3/17	Considerable activity by enemy T.M's artillery & machineguns for two weeks day. Several volleys of fire on defence heavily shelled by enemy at 10 A.M. Today kipped in trenches by T.M. Relief unwritten	AHA

night 11/3/17 Relief unwritten

AB Killian. Miller hulls.

1247 W 3290 200,000 (B) 8/14 J.B.C. & A. Forms/C. 2118/II.

Army Form C. 2118.

2/4 Lincolns SECRET

February 1917

WAR DIARY
or
INTELLIGENCE SUMMARY
(Erase heading not required.)

Instructions regarding War Diaries and Intelligence Summaries are contained in F.S. Regs, Part II. and the Staff Manual respectively. Title pages will be prepared in manuscript.

Hour, Date, Place		Summary of Events and Information	Remarks and references to Appendices
SOUTHAMPTON	2/2/17 17.30	Embarked for FRANCE on S.S. LYDIA	WD
do	do 19.15	Sailed – good evening	WD
LE HAVRE	24/2/17 7.30	Disembarked – marched to Docks Rest Camp – weather fine	WD
do	do 19.00	Entrained at Gare des MARCHANDISES – weather fine	WD
SALEUX	25/2/17 16.30	Detrained & marched to billets at VERS for the night – one company W.D. in SALEUX – weather fine but roads very bad. Transport preceded by separate route.	WD
VERS	26/2/17 9.30	Arrived by march route to FOUENCAMPS where billeted for the night. Weather very dull but roads very bad. Transport proceeded by separate route to FOUENCAMPS.	WD
FOUENCAMPS	27/2/17 9.00	Proceeded by march route to RAYONVILLERS. Roads good – no casualties. Weather fine. Accommodated in fields huts & tents.	WD
RAYONVILLERS	27/2/17	Roads – paid men – foot had seen rifle & gas helmet inspections. Weather fine	WD
do	1/3/17	Company & Battalion Training carried out. Weather fine.	WD
do	2/3/17	Company & Battalion Training carried out. Special training in Box Respirator	Best
do	3/3/17	J.O. Adjt. & Officers Maintain N.C.Os & 1 Platoon per Coy left for entrainment at train in fort line trenches	WD
do	4/3/17	Sunday. Church Parade in A.M.	WD
do	5/3/17	Bn. entrained at station to FOUCAUCOURT by march route en route to the Trenches	WD

A W Stevens Lt Col Commdg

WAR DIARY 1/4 LINCOLNS

or

INTELLIGENCE SUMMARY

Army Form C. 2118.

(Erase heading not required.)

Hour, Date, Place	Summary of Events and Information	Remarks and references to Appendices
BELLOY 12/3/17	On IVR until 6.15 A.M. Relief remainder of day. Removal during relief. Trenches very bad.	W.M.J.
do 13/3/17	Working parties usual. 320 sent out. 5 casualties (all slight) from Shrapnel.	W.M.J.
do 14/3/17	Working parties on Inverness trench. B & D Coys R.T. den Nord. Heavy shelling during night about 2 A.M. magazine at 8.30 A.M. to 10.30 A.M. no casualties.	W.M.J.
do 15/3/17	Working parties as usual. 1 one casualty. Enemy quiet.	W.M.J.
do 16/3/17	General warning as to probable withdrawal of enemy. Rather very quiet. Working parties as usual.	W.M.J.
do 17/3/17 2 A.M. 7 A.M.	Two raids carried out simultaneously N & J of ESTREES - VILLERS CARBONNEL Road. In each case ascertained that enemy had evacuated front line position.	W.M.J.
do 12 N.	Enemy reported to be clear East of River SOMME. 2nd stood by in Reserve.	W.M.J.
do 18/3/17	2nd Lincolns brought up in support & this point in Reserve.	W.M.J.
do 19/3/17.	On working parties repairing main ESTREES - VILLERS CARBONNEL	W.M.J.
do 20/3/17.	Roads - Track Trenches to BELLOY. See for 19/3/17.	W.M.J.

W.B. Johnson Maj.
2/Lt 1/4 Lincs

WAR DIARY 1/4 Lincolns or INTELLIGENCE SUMMARY

Army Form C. 2118.

(Erase heading not required.)

Hour, Date, Place	Summary of Events and Information	Remarks and references to Appendices
BELLOY : 22/3/17.	Relieved by 2/4 Monmouth Jn to Fos & marched into rest at BOIS ST MARTIN 1½ miles W. of FOUCAUCOURT.	WJW
BOIS ST MARTIN: 23/3/17.	Rested & bathed.	WJW
do : 24/3/17.	Working parties on Railway at BOIS TRIANGULAIRE on main road.	WJW
do : 24/3/17.	Moved up into rear part of the line. Stopped en route in dugouts at BELLOY for night.	WJW
BELLOY : 25/3/17.	Marched BELLOY to LE MESNIL. Took up outpost line through CATELET.	WJW
LE MESNIL : 26/3/17.	Marched LE MESNIL to ROUCY. Took up outpost line in immediate touch with our cavalry screen. Outpost piquets slightly shelled but no casualties. Enemy occupying HERVILLY with snipers & ridge East of it in strength.	WJS
ROUCY : 27/3/17.	Night all quiet. Patrols & standing piquets fired on at daybreak from HERVILLY & one man killed.	WJS
7 P.M.	Relieved with C Coy & 2 Coys 1/4 Lincolns not holding Posts on.	WJW
10 P.M.	Patrols in touch with enemy piquet-fired on near HERVILLY to his loss.	A.W. Johnson Maj OC 1/4 Lincolns

WAR DIARY 2/4 LINCOLNS
or
INTELLIGENCE SUMMARY

Army Form C. 2118.

(Erase heading not required.)

Hour, Date, Place	Summary of Events and Information	Remarks and references to Appendices
Bovery 28/3/17	Relief previously arranged for today postponed. Wiring slightly in front on Coy on Coy's front. One casualty. Repaired at Ronssoy.	
do 29/3/17 10¹⁵pm	Watercarts shelled while drawing water - one casualty. Wire continued by night on Coys front. D Coy orders to evacuate Hervilly until Bayonet 1st messengers to hold it out as per Relieve.	
do 30/3/17 4pm	Project returned showing drawn fire from every part of front end - suffered one casualty. Decided to not the village that night - and not went. Proposed operation amended owing to larger operation being carried out the following day.	
2pm		
do 31/3/7	Moved by two that 1/5 Leicester (if necessary) is attacked, which was successful. No order were issued to move etc for 1/5 no unusual movement. Carried no returns first night	
	Bivouacs that night	

A.W. Johnson
O.C. 2/4 Lincolns

WAR DIARY or INTELLIGENCE SUMMARY

Army Form C. 2118.

Hour, Date, Place	Summary of Events and Information	Remarks and references to Appendices
1/4/17. BOUZY.	Moved station by march route to ROISEL.	177/59
2/4/17 - ROISEL. 7.30 PM	Halted one line & leaving ROISEL.	
	Stood by in support of 9th Brigade who were making an attack.	
3/4/17. do 12.15 AM	Stood down	
1st AM	One Company called out to march but recalled to rest at	
	& returned at 6 AM.	
	Working parties out as usual but recalled to rest as BROSSE WOOD	
	10.15 A.M. an attack on FERVAQUE FM & BROSSE WOOD	
	ordered that night.	
6.45 P.M.	Pushed forward to N.S. of HESBECOURT under cover	
8.15 P.M.	Buff Co's moved to be in position for assault. 1/A-D in firing line C	
	moving forward ready for assault. 1/A-D in firing line C	
	& D in support, B in reserve.	
9.15 P.M.	Barrage lifted & attack rushed & except by lying still five	
	was no 15 - 30 yds. the enemy opened with MGs rifle & machine guns	
	Heavy enemy fire opened with 77 mm H.E.s and minenwerfer	
	against.	
4/4/17. 11.30 P.M.	Withdrawal ordered	
2 AM	Withdrawal completed. Casualties 2/Lt Shaw (1/6 K.O. Cam Rlns)	
	killed & Lieuts (att) R.HAND & C/F McDONALD wounded	
	Killed & others. 36 O.R. killed, wounded & 16 missing.	
	Unit furnished remainder of day	

WAR DIARY or INTELLIGENCE SUMMARY

Army Form C. 2118.

(Erase heading not required.)

T/Lt finish

Instructions regarding War Diaries and Intelligence Summaries are contained in F. S. Regs., Part II. and the Staff Manual respectively. Title pages will be prepared in manuscript.

Hour, Date, Place	Summary of Events and Information	Remarks and references to Appendices
ROISEL 4/4/17	Rested remainder of day	Maps
do " 5/4/17	Ordered forward on C.O. to support line of 48th Divn at TEMPLEUX	Maps
do " 1 A.M.	C Coy sent leaving at 3.45 A.M.	
TEMPLEUX 9 A.M.	Battalion ordered up in support, arrived TEMPLEUX at noon. Took over outpost line between TEMPLEUX & HARGICOURT. Village heavily shelled during afternoon	Maps
do " 6/4/17	Have heavy shelling. B Coy HQ hit — Capt L.L. HARVEY wounded. Casualties for the day 1 Officer wounded 3 O.R. killed and 16 wounded. Patrol which advanced to the German trench NORTH of HARGICOURT shelled out.	Maps
do " 7/4/17	Patrols discovered German Posts N & NE & outskirts of HARGICOURT. No other enemy found there. Patrol take up all day then nothing. Have heavy shelling + post again shelled out of HARGICOURT. Casualties 1 O.R. killed, 6 wounded 1 O.R.	Maps
do " 8/4/17	Patrols established in HARGICOURT during night. Shelled out. Relieved by at time by 1/4 GLOSTERS. Casualties during day 1 O.R. killed 4 D.R. wounded.	Maps

D.K. Shaw Lt Colonel

WAR DIARY or INTELLIGENCE SUMMARY

Army Form C. 2118.

1/4 Lincolns

(Erase heading not required.)

Instructions regarding War Diaries and Intelligence Summaries are contained in F.S. Regs., Part II. and the Staff Manual respectively. Title pages will be prepared in manuscript.

Hour, Date, Place	Summary of Events and Information	Remarks and references to Appendices
TEMPLEUX 9/4/17. 6 AM - 9 PM	Enemy reported to be withdrawing. Patrols sent out and reported that enemy were still in occupation of trenches.	
12 ND P.M.	A party of about 20 enemy seen to retire from trenches near FERMAQU=FM	
5 P.M.	Authority received from Brigade to occupy enemy trenches. Entered trenches north of FERMAQUIE Jm through Ruang to captured trenches up to HARGICOURT. VILLERET road — Thence JV & west of HARGICOURT.	
do. 10/4/17. 2.25 AM	3 O.R. wounded. Partial relief complete at this hour Partial taken over by 2/5 Lincolns.	
do. 11/4/17. 7 AM	Rest of remainder of day Stood by in support of 2/5 Lincolns who attacked but were forced to withdraw.	
9.30 AM	Stood down but remained ready to move at short notice.	
do 12/4/17	Working parties out by day & night no made & trench clearing & trenching new position by night. 10 O.R. O/Rs moved into ROISEL to billets.	
do 13/4/17	do for previous day. One O.R. killed & one missed by collapse of a house in ROISEL.	
do 14/4/17	do for previous day. One officer (2/Lt H. H. Holmes) slightly injured by fall of a trench of trench on 12/4/17. Two O.R.'s working parties wounded by shrapnel.	
do 15/4/17.	Working parties officer cleaning up during forenoon & water remainder of day as were ordered to support an expected attack on VILLERET that night.	

A.W. Vernon Lt Col Comdg
1/4 Lincolns

WAR DIARY or INTELLIGENCE SUMMARY

Army Form C. 2118.

1/4 Sherwoods

Hour, Date, Place	Summary of Events and Information	Remarks and references to Appendices
TEMPLEUX 16/9/17	Battalion HQ moved temporarily to operations to CROSS WOOD N°1 - 2500 yds E of South of TEMPLEUX. In pursuit of GPW attack successful the hostile post called the NEST was captured with 10 prisoners + casualties on other flanks.	Ack
do 17/9/17	Returned HQ to Bn of 6.30 AM under the warning order most at N end of VILLERET & in vicinity of VILLERET - HARGICOURT received new orders received for attack on Bunny N of VILLERET on night of 18/9.	Ack
do 18/9/17	Three Platoons of B Coy withdrawn from line to rest. Reconnoitred the position for following night's operations.	Ack
do 19/9/17	Bn HQ Temporarily moved to GRANDE PRIEL WOOD N. Dispositions as under. Firing line - Support A+C Cos. Front B in Support. General Reserve & carrying party. Front B Cov (4p + 1 platoon) known R Coy (4p + 1 platoon) moved from Bn HQ @ 9.15 p.m. night to dark that 9/5 position. Enemy bombardment S of Runnery Railway. very slow progress was made. Bn HQ received to be in occupied by 2.45 AM. 19/9/17. Orders received to withdraw was done after daylight. The withdrawal take place in Runnery before daylight. Two ports on entrenchment were found to be untenable. Forced to withdraw under daylight heavy fire & under cover of our barrage. Casualties 1 OR missing believed killed, 9 ORs wounded. Relieved that night by 2/7 Sherwood Foresters.	Ack

A.H. Flannery Lt Colonel
1/4 Sherwoods

WAR DIARY
or
INTELLIGENCE SUMMARY 2/4 Lincolns

Army Form C. 2118.

(Erase heading not required.)

Hour, Date, Place		Summary of Events and Information	Remarks and references to Appendices
ROISEL	20/4/17	Disposition in Rest – A. + D. Co's R.M.Stores Transport at HAMELET B + C Co's HQ at ROISEL. Working parties 150 strong formed. Similar working parties. Bathing proceeding concurrently.	
do	21/4/17		
do	22/4/17	do do previous day. Refitting as fast as possible. little training done.	
do	23/4/17	do do previous day. Specialist training etc.	
do	24/4/17	Inspection by C.O. of B + D Companys. Not such large working parties this day.	
do	25/4/17	Inspection by Maj Gen Romer wounded 59 Division & heads	
do	26/4/17	head working parties. Specialist Training	
do	27/4/17 4 PM	Orders by Brigade recvd to 178 (Sherwood) Infty Bde who were carrying out an attack in Quarry S.E. of HARGICOURT + on WOLEM-FW East of HARGICOURT.	
	7.30 PM	Orders up to QUELLIES WOODS. When in reserve – informed that Quarry had been taken but not COLOGNE Fm – Casualties heavy.	
	7 PM	Orders received for situation B 80% 60 under & duly despatched:- A Coy to hold Quarry + Railway embankment in relief of 2/6 Sherwood B Coy to hold trenches West of Quarry in relief of " " A Coy in Bn reserve nr RUELIEF WOOD D Coy in Bde reserve East of Quarry Casualties 11/Temp/Pbrgnt A.M.S. Palmer, Machine Gun W.R.S. Yarwich 11/L (K/AB 8008) 2/L/L Preston 1/L. Killed 9 O.R. 2/L M.G. Godfrey + 16 O.R. wounded

Army Form C. 2118.

WAR DIARY
or
INTELLIGENCE SUMMARY
(Erase heading not required.)

2/4 LINCOLNS

Hour, Date, Place	Summary of Events and Information	Remarks and references to Appendices
RUEILLES WOODS 28/4/17		
10 p.m.	On position as before - Casualties 3 ORs wounded.	
	Whole of B Coy moved into line + 3 Platoons	
	info support in Quarry West of HARGICOURT.	
	A.T.C. out all night wiring in vicinity of D Coy front.	
29/4/17	All fairly quiet. Though persistent shelling of Quarry + B.T.	WMc
	+ Coys fronts.	ORs
30/4/17 3 A.M.	B + C Coys relieved by 1st S.Foresters, A + D Coys returned to	
	JEANCOURT + C Coy to RUEILLES WOODS	ORs
do 4 A.M.	A + C Coys relieved by 2/6 S.Foresters + moved with HQrs to JEANCOURT	WMc
JEANCOURT 6 A.M.	where took over from 4/5 S.Staffs Regt.	
do 9 p.m.	A.T.C. Coy to various parties and mended supports on the line.	

O.W.S. Johnson W Colonel
2/4 Lincoln

1247 W 8299 200,000 (E) 8/14 J.B.C.&A. Forms/C. 2118/11.

ORIGINAL

SECRET

1/4 LINCOLNS.

Army Form C. 2118.

WAR DIARY
or
INTELLIGENCE SUMMARY

(Erase heading not required.)

Instructions regarding War Diaries and Intelligence Summaries are contained in F. S. Regs., Part II. and the Staff Manual respectively. Title pages will be prepared in manuscript.

Hour, Date, Place	Summary of Events and Information	Remarks and references to Appendices
JEAWCOURT 1/5/17	Remarks 2 NCOs working parties went out to Roisel...	
do 2/5/17	... LE VERGUIER ... A.K.M. A.D	
do 3/5/17	Whitmath .... party ...	
do 4/5/17	... parade day. 2/Lt C.M. EVERETT reported in duty	
do 5/5/17	... parade day ...	G.D.F.
LE VERGUIER 6/5/17	The Bn relieved 2/5 Lincs Regt. in Bde. night sub-sector. 2 Coys on outpost line – G.32.c.3.8. to G.25.d.0.9 facing N.E. 2 Coys on Divisional line of resistance – L.34.b.q.8. to R.5.C.3.1. Bn H.Q. L.33.d.3.3. Map ref:- FRANCE 62c N.E. 62c S.E. 62c N.W. 62c S.W. Contact established with 2/5 Leics Regt. on left and LANCS FUSILIERS (35th DIV) on right. Capt. & Adjt. W.M. PHILLIPS went in to Hospital with Trench fever. Lieut G.D. FOX was appointed acting Adjutant. Strengthening of defences on outpost line commenced.	
do 7/5/17	Wiring in front of outpost line and defences of transport continued by night. 1 O.R. killed by shell fire on Div line & ricochets.	G.D.F.
do 8/5/17		G.D.F.
do 9/5/17	As for previous day	G.D.F.
do 10/5/17	2nd Lieut A.L. DIGB and 2nd Lieut C.A.J. ANDREWS reported for duty from BASE REINFORCEMENTS. the former having posted to "C" the latter to "A" Coy. 2nd Lieut DIBB accidentally wounded him self and with a revolver shot and was admitted to Hospital Capt. C.L. HARVEY died of wounds in London Hospital.	G.D.F.

Army Form C. 2118.

WAR DIARY
or
INTELLIGENCE SUMMARY
(Erase heading not required.)

Instructions regarding War Diaries and Intelligence Summaries are contained in F. S. Regs., Part II. and the Staff Manual respectively. Title pages will be prepared in manuscript.

Hour, Date, Place	Summary of Events and Information	Remarks and references to Appendices
LE VERGUIER 11/5/17	Wiring in front of outpost line continued at night. Scouts and patrols visited NEW WOOD in E.25.c. in preparation for a raid on enemy party reported in wood.	G.S.F.
do. 12/5/17	Casualties during day 2. O.R. wounded. Raid on NEW WOOD carried out by "B" Coy. A small party of enemy was surprised and withdrew. We made no captures, but identification was established of 73rd FUSILIER Regt. by means of captured equipment. Attempt to establish small post in wood failed, the post being worked out by enemy infested part of enemy. Casualty 1 O.R. wounded. Capt. E.T. HICKS died in hospital of cerebro-spinal meningitis.	G.S.F.
do. 13/5/17	Two small patrols visited NEW WOOD with the object of securing prisoners, but finding strong enemy posts in occupation, withdrew. Wiring continued.	G.S.F.
do 14/5/17	Officers of Cavalry Bde. reconnoitred our sub. sector. Wiring Cos. to wood. 2nd Lieut. L.W.THAIN reported for duty, and was posted to "C" Coy.	G.S.F.
do 15/5/17	Bn. relieved by 7th DRAGOON GUARDS, who took over outpost line, and by 9th HODSON'S HORSE who occupied Div. line of resistance.	G.S.F.
VRAIGNES 16/5/17	Relief complete 2.00 a.m. when Coy. marched independently to VRAIGNES and went into billets	G.S.F.
do. 17/5/17	Re-rested	G.S.F.
do. 18/5/17	Training in all branches of work commenced: especially control by platoon commanders	G.S.F.
do 19/5/17	As for previous day	G.S.F.

A.B. Johnson Lt.Col. Comm'dg
2/4 Berkshire Regt.

WAR DIARY or INTELLIGENCE SUMMARY

(Erase heading not required.)

Army Form C. 2118.

Hour, Date, Place	Summary of Events and Information	Remarks and references to Appendices
VRAIGNES 20/5/17	Bde. Church parade on ground between BIAS WOOD and STABLE WOOD - P.15.a.6.8. G.O.C. 59th Div. presented a card to Cpl. H. LITTLE for gallant conduct on 3/4 April near FERVAQUE FARM and to card to No. 202738 Pte H. LEA for gallant conduct on 18/19 April in the neighbourhood of VIMY RIDGE.	G.S.F.
do 21/5/17	Training continued	G.S.F.
do 22/5/17	As for previous day.	G.S.F.
do 23/5/17	Brigade Parade. B.G.C. 177th Inf. Bde. presented No. 201286 Sergt. FARNSWORTH with D.C.M. for showing great coolness and gallantry on 3/4 April 1917 near FERVAQUE FARM. 2nd Lieut. P. L. SQUIRRELL reported for duty and was posted to "C" Coy.	G.S.F.
do 24/5/17	Training continued	G.S.F.
do 25/5/17	Bn. left VRAIGNES by march - route via BOUCLY, TEMPLEUX-LA-FOSSE, AIZECOURT-LE-BAS, NURLU, arriving at EQUANCOURT, where camp was pitched distance of march 12 miles. The day was extremely hot and several men fell out en route. The Divisional Commander congratulated the Bn. on the excellent march discipline of men as they reached camp.	G.S.F.
EQUANCOURT 26/5/17	Training. Football match with 2nd LINCOLNS, who were in rest at NURLU. 2nd Lieut. A.P.O. WARD reported for duty with Bn. and was posted to "B" Coy.	G.S.F.
do 27/5/17	Brigade Church Parade.	G.S.F.

W.B. Johnson Lt. Col. Comndg.
2/4 Bn. Lincs Regt.

WAR DIARY
or
INTELLIGENCE SUMMARY

(Erase heading not required.)

Army Form C. 2118.

Instructions regarding War Diaries and Intelligence Summaries are contained in F. S. Regs., Part II. and the Staff Manual respectively. Title pages will be prepared in manuscript.

Hour, Date, Place	Summary of Events and Information	Remarks and references to Appendices
EQUANCOURT 28/5/17	Tug of war contest with 2nd Lincoln. On left eant at EQUANCOURT for GOUZEAUCOURT WOOD, where Bn H.Q was established – also "A" & "D" Coys. – "B" & "C" Co intermediate line	9/5F
GOUZEAUCOURT WOOD 29/5/17	Improvement of cover in wood and in immediate line. Digging by night on No 1 communication trench behind intermediate line and trench line.	9/5F
30/5/17	As for previous day. 2 Coys in a trench & a line relieved by 3/5 Linc. Regt. and withdrawn to GOUZEAUCOURT WOOD where the Bn was established in Brigade Support.	9/5F
31/5/17	Bn H.Q moved from Q29.a.1.2 to Q22.c.2.3 A Coy worked by night in front line under instruction from O.C. 2/5 Leics Regt, remainder of Bn deepened No 1 communication trench	9/5F

W Gordon Doar Major
f Gordon Col Comndg
f 2/4 Bn Linc Regt

1247 W 3299 200,000 (E) 8/14 J.B.C. & A. Forms/C. 2118/11.

SECRET

ORIGINAL

Army Form C. 2118.

WAR DIARY
2/4th Lincoln Regt.
INTELLIGENCE SUMMARY

(Erase heading not required.)

JUNE 1917 Vol 1

Instructions regarding War Diaries and Intelligence Summaries are contained in F. S. Regs, Part II. and the Staff Manual respectively. Title pages will be prepared in manuscript.

Hour, Date, Place		Summary of Events and Information	Remarks and references to Appendices
GOUZEAUCOURT WOOD	1.6.17	Bn in support. 3 Coys under instruction from R.E. officer digging communication trenches from front to intermediate line.	G.S.F. SHEET 57CSE
do.	2.6.17	As for previous day. Lieut E.G.W. KNOX went into hospital - trench fever suspected. Information received that Capt. W.M. PHILLIPS was transferred to England 24.5.17 and struck off the strength.	G.S.F.
do.	3.6.17	Church Parade at DESSART WOOD, when Cpl. J. THURLBY was presented with the Military Medal by the Divisional General for gallant conduct on the night 3/4th April 1917 near FERVAQUE FARM.	G.S.F.
do.	4.6.17	Working parties as for previous night.	G.S.F.
do.	5.6.17	As for previous day.	G.S.F.
do.	6.6.17	As for previous day. 2nd Lieut. GALE appointed acting Intelligence officer. Lieut W.E. Carter reported as transferred to England 26.5.17 and struck off the strength.	G.S.F.
do.	7.6.17	Bn relieved the 2/5 Bn Lincs Regt in Divisional Right Sector - left sub-sector of the Brigade - night 6/7th 8 - Relief complete 12.50 a.m. C and D Coys front line 'C' Coy. Q.12.a.7.5 - Q.12.b.1.5 with advanced post at Q.6.d.2.0 and Q.12.6.5.8 'D' Coy Q.12.6.0.5 - Q.12.6.6.0 with one advanced post at Q.12.6.8.6. 'B' Coy. in close support 'A' Coy in intermediate line Bn.H.Q. - S.W. of BEAUCAMP at Q.17.8.9.6. Lieut.Col. returned from command by Officers Conference at Fluxecourt.	G.S.F.

A.M. Athern. Lieut-Col. Commdg:
2/4 Bn Lincs. Regt.

WAR DIARY
INTELLIGENCE SUMMARY
(Erase heading not required.)

Army Form C. 2118.

Instructions regarding War Diaries and Intelligence Summaries are contained in F. S. Regs., Part II. and the Staff Manual respectively. Title pages will be prepared in manuscript.

Place	Hour, Date	Summary of Events and Information	Remarks and references to Appendices
BEAUCAMP	8.6.17.	Two officer patrols proceeded to German advanced posts with object of reconnoitring enemy wire. One patrol under 2nd Lieut. EVERETT was fired on from an isolated German rifle pit but suffered no casualties. Useful information as to height and depth of wire was obtained.	G.S.F.
"	9.6.17.	Trenches very wet owing to heavy thunderstorm and absence of drainage system. Listening patrols report that the Germans have thickened their wire in front of their rifle pits.	G.S.F.
"	10.6.17.	Improvement of trenches. Many splinter proof dug-outs completed in the front and intermediate lines. 2 officer patrols sent out to report on the condition of the BEAUCAMP — RIBECOURT road.	G.S.F.
"	11.6.17.	Wiring in front of advanced posts. Communication trenches from forward posts to front line begun.	G.S.F.
"	12.6.17.	As for previous day.	G.S.F.
"	13.6.17.	2nd Lieut. J.W. Dunne in charge of a fighting patrol made useful reconnaissance but was not successful in coming into contact with enemy patrol. Orders received that (front line) 50 forward posts were to be joined up. Trench accordingly taped out by C. and D. Coys.	G.S.F. G.S.F.
"	14.6.17.	Work between front line posts continued, though our working parties were harassed by M.G. fire.	G.S.F.
"	15.6.17.	At 2.30 a.m an enemy patrol crept close to our No. 3 post ("C"Coy). They were driven off by Lewis Gun and rifle fire. They sustained casualties undoubtedly, but the search for their killed or wounded proved fruitless, though discarded German rifles and stick bombs were saved. Our casualties 2 O.R. killed. 3 O.R. wounded. A.M. Khuwm Lieut- Colonel Comm'dg. 2/4 B'n Lines Regt.	G.S.F.

Army Form C. 2118.

WAR DIARY
—or—
INTELLIGENCE SUMMARY
(Erase heading not required.)

Instructions regarding War Diaries and Intelligence Summaries are contained in F.S. Regs., Part II. and the Staff Manual respectively. Title pages will be prepared in manuscript.

Hour, Date, Place	Summary of Events and Information	Remarks and references to Appendices
BEAUCAMP 16.6.17	Bn. H.Q. moved into sunken road S.E. of BEAUCAMP at 1 a.m. The Bn was ordered to carry out a raid on the German trenches on night of 16th/17th June with the object of capturing prisoners. Raiding Party - Capt. A.G. Hooper 2nd Lieut R.B. Winshurst 2nd Lieut J.W. Durance 2nd Lieut C.A.S. Everett 'D' Coy 20 Other Ranks 'C' Coy 20 " " 'C' Coy 40 " " It was proposed that there should be two points of entry into the enemy's trenches, each party consisting of 1 officer and 20 O.R. A covering party consisting of 1 officer and 20 O.R. was to cover the withdrawal - after the object was achieved. The blacking of faces and usual precautions against identification were adopted by raiding party. Two Bangalore Torpedoes were carried by each party ordered to enter the trenches. The raiding party left No. 3 Post at 11 p.m. and proceeded according to plan to within 50 yards	G/SF
17.6.17	of the enemy wire, where they saw what turned out to be a German battle patrol starting out. Our men waited in the long grass for the enemy to approach within close range, when they opened rapid fire. A pitched battle ensued for a few minutes, in which bombs were made freely by both sides. The result was that the German patrol retired after sustaining severe casualties, leaving two prisoners in our hands; one of these died from wounds before reaching the R.A.P.; the other was unwounded.	G/SF

A.W. Polwin   Lieut. Colonel Command[ing]
2/4 Bn Lincs Regt.

WAR DIARY
or
INTELLIGENCE SUMMARY.
(Erase heading not required.)

Army Form C. 2118.

Hour, Date, Place	Summary of Events and Information	Remarks and references to Appendices
BEAUCAMP 17.6.17 (cont)	This prisoner was of the 1918 class, and had only just joined the Regiment — The 31st I.R. Thus the object of the raid — identification of the unit on this front — was attained, and a congratulatory message was in due course received from the Corps Commander. Estimated casualties of the enemy. 30 killed and wounded. Our casualties. Lieut C.A.S. EVERETT died of wounds. 1 O.R. killed. 3 O.R. wounded. The Bn was relieved by the 2/5 Lincs. Regt.	9/5F.
DESSART WOOD 18.6.17	Relief complete 1.50 a.m. The Bn in Brigade reserve at Dessart Wood. 2nd LIEUT W.S. OWSTON and 2nd LIEUT J.E. ROGERS reported for duty and were both posted to "D" Coy. Bn went to dig in LINCOLN AVENUE i.e. C.T. between Braunfine and intermediate line.	9/5F.
" 19.6.17	Digging as for previous day.	9/5F.
" 20.6.17	The B.G.C. having gone on leave, Lieut Col. A.B. Johnson takes command of the Brigade. Major H.G. Dean in command of the Bn. Digging as for previous day.	9/5F.
" 21.6.17	Brigade into Division of Reserve. Bn took over the Camp vacated by 2/5 Sherwood Foresters.	9/5F.
EQUANCOURT 22.6.17	Bn rests.	9/5F.

M.R. Johnson Lieut-Colonel Commdg.
2/4 Bn Lincs Regt.

Army Form C. 2118.

WAR DIARY
or
INTELLIGENCE SUMMARY.
(Erase heading not required.)

Instructions regarding War Diaries and Intelligence Summaries are contained in F.S. Regs., Part II. and the Staff Manual respectively. Title pages will be prepared in manuscript.

Hour, Date, Place	Summary of Events and Information	Remarks and references to Appendices
EQUANCOURT 23.6.17	Brigade Parade, at which Divisional General presented cards for gallant conduct on the night of 16th/17th to the following N.C.O.s and men of the Bn:- 102352 Sgt. Kingwood F.C., 201027 Sgt. Northing W.H., 200604 Pte. Lilley H., 201707 Pte. Pacey F., 202732 Pte. Glasspool A., 201860 Pte. Dawson W.S., 202571 Pte. Huggin F.C.	G.S.F.
24.6.17	Brigade Church Parade.	G.S.F.
25.6.17	Training in accordance with system laid down in S.S.143.	G.S.F.
26.6.17	Musketry on 30 yards range.	G.S.F.
27.6.17	As for previous day. Battalion Sports.	G.S.F.
28.6.17 }	As for previous day.	
29.6.17 }	Brigade Sports.	
30.6.17	Brigade Rifle Meeting on 30 yards range.	G.S.F.

W.B. Johnson. Lieut-Colonel
Commdg. 2/4 Bn. Lines Regt.

SECRET.

2/4 Bn Lines Regt

WAR DIARY
INTELLIGENCE SUMMARY

Original July 1917

Army Form C. 2118.

Hour, Date, Place	Summary of Events and Information	Remarks and references to Appendices
EQUANCOURT 1.7.17	Lieut-Col A.B. Johnson still in command of the Brigade. The 2/5 N. Staffs. took over our camp at EQUANCOURT. We relieved the 2/5 S. Staffs. in the left Divisional sector. Right of Brigade and sector. A & B Coys front line. C. Coy support line. D. Coy reserve line.	G.S.F. Ref. 57 C. S.E. France
BEAUCAMP 2.7.17	Relief complete 1.15 a.m. though 1 Officer and 4 O.R. of Stafford patrol which had encountered enemy patrol in BOAR COPSE, had not yet returned. It transpired that the officer and 3 O.R. had been killed. The remaining man was wounded and was brought in during the day. A patrol went out at dusk in the hopes of finding in the dead bodies; this they failed to do — casualties 2 O.R. slightly wounded. We sent out a small party at midday, including stretcher bearers, who brought back the bodies of the officer and 2 O.R. of the Staffords, also the body of a German N.C.O. killed in the same encounter.	G.S.F. G.S.F.
" 3.7.17		G.S.F.
" 4.7.17	2nd Lt G.W. Willis and 18 O.R. started out at dusk to reconnoitre German defences, but returned without encountering the enemy and without obtaining information of any value.	G.S.F.

A.B. Johnson Lieut-Colonel
Commanding 2/4 Bn Lines Regt.

SECRET

2/4 Bn Lincs Regt.

Original

WAR DIARY
or
INTELLIGENCE SUMMARY.

Army Form C. 2118.

July 1917

(Erase heading not required.)

Instructions regarding War Diaries and Intelligence Summaries are contained in F. S. Regs., Part II and the Staff Manual respectively. Title pages will be prepared in manuscript.

Place	Hour, Date	Summary of Events and Information	Remarks and references to Appendices
BEAU CAMP	5.7.17	Lieut. Col. A. B. Johnson resumed command of the Bn. Lieut Wilmshurst and 2nd Lieut Gale took out a strong patrol at dusk and brought back useful information about enemy's defences beyond BON R. COPSE and the Ravine. Bn relieved by 2/5 Lincn Regt.	G.P.F. Ref. France 57 C. S.E. 57 C. 57 C. S.W.
NEUVILLE	6.7.17	Relief complete 12.15 a.m. Bn. took over camp vacated by 2/5 Lincs Regt at NEUVILLE. Lieut. Col. A.B. Johnson on Cmdn and Sny Course at Chatham. Major H.G. Dean ian. B. in command	G.P.F. 57 C. S.E. 57 C. G.P.F.
"	7.7.17.	As Bn. in Brigade reserve we supplied working parties for completing O.T.Ls to intermediate line Capt H. Ward	G.P.F.
"	8.7.17.	in command of the Bn. As for previous day. Inspection of camp by Divisional General, who expressed himself as thoroughly satisfied with its condition.	G.P.F.
"	9.7.17.	59th Division relieved by 58th Division	G.P.F.
BARASTRE	10.7.17.	Bn relieved by 2/7 Bn London Regt. We left camp at 8.30 a.m. and proceeded by route march to camp at 0.16.d. near BARASTRE, where the whole Brigade came into camp during the day.	G.P.F. G.P.F.
"	11.7.17.	Section in camp continued under R.E. instruction. Capt. C.J. Monson returned to duty from hospital	G.P.F. G.P.F.

A.B. Johnson Lieut Colonel
Comdg, 2/4 Bn Lin. Regt.

SECRET 2/4 Bn Lincs Regt   Original

Army Form C. 2118.

WAR DIARY
or
INTELLIGENCE SUMMARY.
July 1917

(Erase heading not required.)

Instructions regarding War Diaries and Intelligence Summaries are contained in F.S. Regs., Part II. and the Staff Manual respectively. Title pages will be prepared in manuscript.

Hour, Date, Place	Summary of Events and Information	Remarks and references to Appendices
BARASTRE 12.7.17.	Training commenced. Bn area 0.17 a.b.c. Area for Trench to trench attack 0.21.b.	57 C.S.W. 57 C. Reference 57 C.S.W 57 C
13.7.17.	Training continued.	G.S.F.
14.7.17.	First day's musketry on 30 yards range.	G.S.F.
15.7.17.	Brigade Church Parade, when The Divisional Commander presented the Military Cross to 2nd Lieut. F.W. DURANCE for gallant conduct on the night of 16th/17th June during a raid on enemy's trenches near BEAUCAMP. Company Commanders visited the SOMME battlefield.	G.S.F.
16.7.17.	Musketry and individual training. Sergeants' men completed.	G.S.F.
17.7.17.	Inoculation. Regimental Canteen opened under supervision of Capt. Harris C.F.	G.S.F.
18.7.17.	Training suspended owing to inoculation.	G.S.F.
19.7.17.	The Brigadier General presented the D.C.M. to Sergt. BURGESS for gallant conduct during the raid on the night of 16th/17th June afforded 2nd Lieut. Durance M.C. afforded Brigade musketry officer. Trench to Trench attack practised.	G.S.F.

A.B. Johnson Lieut. Colonel
Comdg. 2/4 Bn Lincs Regt

SECRET 2/4 Bn Lincs Regt. Original

Army Form C. 2118.

Instructions regarding War Diaries and Intelligence
Summaries are contained in F.S. Regs., Part II
and the Staff Manual respectively. Title pages
will be prepared in manuscript.

WAR DIARY
or
INTELLIGENCE SUMMARY.
(Erase heading not required.)

July 1917

Hour, Date, Place	Summary of Events and Information	Remarks and references to Appendices
BARASTRE 20.7.17	Inspection of Camp by Divisional General. Very favourable report.	G.S.F. Ref. France 57.C.S.W. 57.C.
" 21.7.17	Practice Trench to Trench attack. Divisional Sports. 1st Prize won by the Bn.	G.S.F.
" 22.7.17	Brigade Church Parade.	G.S.F.
" 23.7.17	Brigade Trench to Trench attack. 2/4 Bn and 2/5 Bn Lincs Regt. assaulting Bns. 2 Objectives. Teat Fog method.	G.S.F.
" 24.7.17	Individual training - Musketry on 30 yards range.	G.S.F.
" 25.7.17	Lieut. Col. A.B. Johnson returned from leave and took over command of Bn. from Capt. H. Ward.	G.S.F.
" 26.7.17	Individual Training. Divisional Musketry Competition. The 2/4 Lincs Regt. obtained the greatest number of prizes in the Division.	G.S.F.
" 27.7.17	Divisional Tactical Exercise No.1 Trench to Trench attack with 3 objectives on battlefield between SAILLY-SAILLISEL and LE TRANSLOY. 178th Inf. Bde on right - 177th Inf. Bde on left. 2/4 Lincs Regt. right Bn. and sector 2/5 Lincs Regt. left Bn. and sector in support and assaulting Bns. 2/4 and 2/5 Lincs Regt. Final objective enemy 1st - 2nd system consolidated between 176th Inf. Bde mark though to capture PROSERPINES TRENCH.	G.S.F.

A.B. Johnson
Lieut Colonel
Comdg. 2/4 Bn Lincs Regt

SECRET. 2/4 Bn Lines Regt. Original.

Army Form C. 2118.

WAR DIARY
or
INTELLIGENCE SUMMARY.

July 1917.

(Erase heading not required.)

Hour, Date, Place	Summary of Events and Information	Remarks and references to Appendices
BARASTRE 28.7.17	Tactical Exercise of previous day repeated by 177th L.f.Bde. Following officers are in present reported for duty with Bn. and were posted as under:- 2nd Lieut. G.S. Lakeman - "C" Coy 2nd Lieut. O.F. Nicholl - "C" Coy 2nd Lieut. T.D.R. Gully - "D" Coy	Ref France 57 C.S.W. 57 C. G.S.F.
29.7.17	Heavy Thunderstorm. No Church Parade.	G.S.F.
30.7.17	Open Warfare attack practised by Companies and Battalion.	G.S.F.
31.7.17	A & D Coys on Field Firing Range near THILLOY. B & C - Bombing throwing Grenades, overhead practice.	G.S.F.

M. Munro
Lieut. Colonel
Commandg 2/4 Bn Lines Regt.

OPERATION ORDERS
by
Lieut Colonel A. B. Johnson.
Comdg. 2/4 "Lincolnshire Regt"

26.7.17.
Ref 1/1 Sy Rd Trench Map

1. On 27th July 1917. The 59th Division will attack the enemy trenches between O.14.f.2 and N36.d.u.3., the 4th and N62 Divisions attacking at same time on right and left. The 176th Inf. Bde will attack on the right & the 177th Inf Bde on the left.
   The 3 objectives are 1.) German front line trench
                        2.) Star trench   "
                        3.) Arcade   "
   These trenches will be consolidated.
   After capture of Arcade Trench the 178th Inf Bde will pass through and consolidate a position in continuation of Kromsten trench and Windmill Mound.
   An Artillery Barrage is shown on attached sketch.
   The attack of the 177th Inf Bde will be made by the 2/5 Lincs Regt on the right & 2/5 Lincs Regt on left, forming line as shown on map.
   2/4 "Leicesters in support
   2/5 "   "   reserve.

2. "The 9/" Lines Regt will attack on a
   2 Coy frontage, with 2 platoons in
   each wave, all Coys being distributed
   in depth.

3. 1st Wave 2 Platoons as per margin will
   form up in British front line trench
   Nos 5 & 9   and will attack first objective.
                          (German front line trench)

4. 2nd Wave Platoons as per margin will
              form up in support trench and
   Nos 2 & 14 will follow 1st wave at a distance
              of 100x and will take 2nd objective

5. 3rd Wave Platoons as per margin will
              form up in A Assembly trenches
   No 1 & 13 and capture 3rd objective.
              2 Trench Mortars will advance with
              this wave as far as 2nd objective,
              where they will await further orders
              from O.C. 9/ Lines Regt
              2 M.Gs of 177th M.G. Coy. will
              advance in 2nd line of this wave
              in far as 3rd objective, and await
              orders from O.C. 9/ Lines Regt.

6. Nos 6 & 10 Platoons as per margin will form
              up in B Assembly trenches and

All watches in Bn will be synchronised on completion of march.

14. R A P

15. Bn H Q

16. Reports to Bn H Q

[signature]
Lieut. Colonel
O/C* Lincoln Regt

26/7/17

will follow after 3rd wave has gone, via C.T. to British front line trench, where they will act as reserves.

7. 4 Spare Lewis Guns will be concentrated at Bn. H.Q. in reserve.

8. 1 Coy 3/5 Leicester Regt will form up in "B" Assembly trenches and will act as a carrying party.

9. 1 N.C.O and 6 sappers will move forward with 3rd wave to assist in consolidating 3rd objective.

10. Each wave on reaching its objective will consolidate. When 3rd objective is gained, scouts will go out immediately and outpost line will also be established.

11. Communication. The Bn S.O. will arrange to lay wires to 1st 2nd and 3rd objectives from B.H.Q.

12. Zero hour 9. AM.

13. The Bn S.O. will call at Bde H.Q at 6.30 AM for synchronisation of watches

CONFIDENTIAL.

WAR DIARY
— of —
INTELLIGENCE SUMMARY.

(Erase heading not required.)

Army Form C. 2118.

Original

2/4 Lincoln Regt.   AUGUST 1917

Instructions regarding War Diaries and Intelligence Summaries are contained in F.S. Regs., Part II and the Staff Manual respectively. Title pages will be prepared in manuscript.

Hour, Date, Place	Summary of Events and Information	Remarks and references to Appendices
BARASTRE 1.8.17.	Divisional Tactical Scheme No 2 cancelled owing to rain. Lectures and Individual training carried out under cover.	9.D.F. 57 C. FRANCE 57 C. S.W.
" 2.8.17.	A wet morning. Programme as for previous day. A draft of 65 O.R. arrived from T.B.D. Capt. Harris C.F. and Lieut Hourn proceeded on leave.	9.D.F.
" 3.8.17.	Tactical exercise carried out based on old battlefield near Fransloy. Lieut-Col. A.B. Johnson in command of 7th/11th 9th. Inf. Bde - Capt. A.H. Clark in command of the Bn. Capt. A.C. Hooper returned from course at 4th Army Infantry School. Lieut. J. Summers R.A.M.C. returned from hospital and resumed duties of medical officer vice Capt. Nisbett who left the unit.	9.D.F.
" 4.8.17.	Lieut E.G.V. Knox went on a course for recognition of aircraft. 2nd Lieut H.E. Godfrey reported for duty with the Bn.	9.D.F.
" 5.8.17.	Brigade Church Parade. 2nd Lieut L.W. Thain attained assistant adjutant. Capt. A.G. Hooper and Lieut. G.D. Fox proceeded on leave. 2nd Lieut J.E. Simpson and 2nd Lieut R. Scott reported for duty, also a draft of 65 O.R. from 9.B.D.	9.D.F.
" 6.8.17.	Divisional Field Day. Lieut Coulson returned from Lewis Gun Course.	

A.M. Johnson Lieut-Colonel
Comm'g 2/4 Bn Lincs Regt.

CONFIDENTIAL

WAR DIARY

Original.

INTELLIGENCE SUMMARY.

(Erase heading not required.)

2/4 Lincoln Regt.

Army Form C. 2118.

August 1917

Hour, Date, Place		Summary of Events and Information	Remarks and references to Appendices
BARASTRE	7.8.17.	Individual Training by Companies	G.S.F. 57 C } FRANCE
"	8.8.17.	As for previous day. Lieut Knox returned from course. 2nd Lieut. H. F. Smith reported for duty. 2nd Lieut A.P.O. Ward returned from hospital	G.S.F. 57 C. S.W. }
"	9.8.17.	Battalion and company training	G.S.F.
"	10.8.17.	As for previous day. 2nd Lieut R.A. Pescod reported for duty	G.S.F.
"	11.8.17.	Divisional Tactical Exercise	G.S.F.
"	12.8.17.	2 Drafts of 47 O.R. and 63 O.R. arrived from I.B.D. Brigade Church Parade	G.S.F.
"	13.8.17.	Battalion and Company training	G.S.F.
"	14.8.17.	Brigade Travel to Trench attack in the morning	G.S.F.
"	15.8.17.	Individual training. Companies now organised on a basis of 4 fighting platoons and 1 training platoon	G.S.F.
"	16.8.17.	A tactical relief in the trenches was carried out by night. our Bn. being relieved by 2/4th Leicesters. Draft of 15 O.R. arrival	G.S.F.
"	17.8.17.	Individual training reported for duty – 2nd Lieuts Hillery, Joynes, Barker. Brigade Races. Several officers rode their chargers in the 5 Furlong flat race but with no success	G.S.F.
"	18.8.17.	Jim, a chestnut pony ridden by Pte. Fox, won the pack pony race open to the Brigade.	G.S.F.

A.M. Johnson Lieut-Colonel
Commdg. 2/4 Bn Linc. Regt.

CONFIDENTIAL.

Army Form C. 2118.

WAR DIARY
INTELLIGENCE SUMMARY.

(Erase heading not required.)

Instructions regarding War Diaries and Intelligence Summaries are contained in F.S. Regs., Part II and the Staff Manual respectively. Title pages will be prepared in manuscript.

Original

2/4 Lincoln Regt. August 1917

Hour, Date, Place	Summary of Events and Information	Remarks and references to Appendices
BARASTRE 19.8.17.	Brigade Church Parade. 2 2 O.R. reinforcements from Base Depot.	G.S.F. 57.C. FRANCE. 57 C.S.W. ALBERT (combined 2 feet) 57.D.SE 57.C.S.W 62.D.NE 62.C.NW
" 20.8.17.	Brigade night march on a company bearing with the assistance of guides carrying lamp-boxes, locality	G.S.F.
" 21.8.17.	O.17. a. and b. Preparation for leaving camp on following morning. By this date practically the whole Battalion was accommodated in Nyssen Huts.	G.S.F.
MILLENCOURT 22.8.17.-	Bn proceeded by march-route and on motor-lorries via BAPAUME - POZIÈRES - ALBERT to MILLENCOURT, each half battalion marching 11 miles and being conveyed on lorries for 11 miles. Sixteenth hot day - 17 men fell out, but all with one exception rejoined before the end of the day.	G.S.F.
" 23.8.17	Individual training	G.S.F.
" 24.8.17	Route-march. Distance 8½ miles. No casualties. Nog Platoon was marching fast competition.	G.S.F.
" 25.8.17	Individual training	G.S.F.
" 26.8.17	Bn Church Parade	G.S.F.
" 27.8.17	Route-march. Distance 9 miles. 2 Casualties. No. 6 Platoon tied with No. 9 Platoon in march-fast.	G.S.F.
" 28.8.17.	Company Platoon and specialist training.	G.S.F.
" 29.8.17	As for previous day. Move to new area postponed for 24 hours.	G.S.F.

A.M. Johnson Lieut. Colonel
Comdg. 2/4 Bn. Lincs Regt.

CONFIDENTIAL

Army Form C. 2118.

WAR DIARY

Original

INTELLIGENCE SUMMARY.

(Erase heading not required.)

2/4 Lincoln Regt - August 1917

Instructions regarding War Diaries and Intelligence Summaries are contained in F. S. Regs., Part II and the Staff Manual respectively. Title pages will be prepared in manuscript.

Hour, Date, Place	Summary of Events and Information	Remarks and references to Appendices
MILLENCOURT 30.8.17	Training as for previous day and preparation for the move. "A" Coy. left billets at 10.15 p.m. for ALBERT, whence they proceeded with the first train to new area to act as detraining party for Brigade Group.	G.O.F. ALBERT (combined sheet) FRANCE HAZEBROUCK 5a. 1/100,000.
MILLENCOURT } 31.8.17 WINNEZEELE }	Bn: (less "A" Coy.) left billets at 5.21 a.m. and proceeded via HAZEBROUCK to PROVEN the detraining station - arrived here 4.45 p.m. - thence by route-march (7½ miles) to WINNEZEELE, where the Bn. went into camp.	G.O.F.

M.B. Johnson
Lieut-Col
Commdg: 2/4 Bn. Linc. Regt.

WAR DIARY
INTELLIGENCE SUMMARY

Army Form C. 2118.

SECRET

2/4 (110201 N REGT

SEPTEMBER 1917   177/59

(Erase heading not required.)

Hour, Date, Place	Summary of Events and Information	Remarks and references to Appendices
WINNEZEELE. 1.9.17	2/Lt S. L. BROMFIELD and 11 other ranks reported morning of 31.8.17 when Bath entrained. Taken on the strength as from today. Lieut Winckworth returned off leave. 2nd Lt O.H. Nicholls returns Lewis Gun Course. Taken on strength.	HAZEBROUCK. 5a FRANCE 1100,0-0-0 1100,0-0-0
2.9.17	2nd Lt. P. MASTERMAN SMITH reports for duty. Taken on strength from 3rd Batn. Church Parade. 2/Lt 2.R. Conbeare returned from leave.	S/B. S/B.
3.9.17	Tactical Exercise.	
4.9.17	Lewis gun training by Companies. 2nd Lt G.W. Willis returned from leave.	S/B.
5.9.17	Lewis gun training by Companies.	S/B.
6.9.17	Individual training by Companies. Tactical exercise for Officers at 5.30pm.	S/B.
7.9.17	Individual training by Companies.	S/B.
8.9.17	Inspection of Batt by G.O.C. 5th Army, General Sir H. de la Gough K.C.B. K.C.V.O. A tactical exercise was arranged in the field and carried out under the direction of Capt M.G.M Gale.	S/B.
9.9.17	Batn Church parade. 2nd Lt G.W. Willis proceeds to POPERINGHE as at Divisional Amusement Officer.	C/B.

H. Gordon Dean Major.
Commanding 2/4 (110201 N) Regt.

WAR DIARY
or
INTELLIGENCE SUMMARY.

(Erase heading not required.)

Army Form C. 2118.

Instructions regarding War Diaries and Intelligence Summaries are contained in F.S. Regs., Part II and the Staff Manual respectively. Title pages will be prepared in manuscript.

Hour, Date, Place		Summary of Events and Information	Remarks and references to Appendices
WINNEZEELE.	10.9.17.	Individual training. Company Tactics in Night marching & night attacks and Patrols.	FRANCE + BELGIUM HAZEBROUCK Sh 1/100,000
"	11.9.17.	Individual training. Capt. C.E.J. Monroe proceeded to ETAPLES as draft Conducting Officer	ShB
"	12.9.17.	Individual training and close order drill. During evening Tactical exercise under Company Commanders. 2/Lt R.E.M. Andrews and 4 other Ranks dispatched to XIX Reinforcement Camp to form part of personnel of 59th Divisional Depot Battn. Medical Officer proceeded on leave. His duties performed temporarily by Lieut E.E. Owens (RAMC) 2/Lt G.S. Bakeman and 2/Lt T.D.R. Crilly proceeded to XIX Corps Inf School on General Course. ShB	ShB
"	13.9.17.	Battn in Tactical Tactics. 2/Lt E.W. Barker returned from Course.	ShB
"	14.9.17.	Company parade for bathing. Individual training as far as bathing permitted.	ShB
"	15.9.17.	Battn took part in Bde tactical Tactics	ShB
"	16.9.17.	Battn. Church parade.	ShB
"	17.9.17.	Individual training. Officer F.C. Robertson and 2/Lt H. Jaques together with 150 other ranks proceeded on a musketry Course to 5th Army Musketry Camp	ShB
"	18.9.17.	Battn in Tactical Tactics. Capt. E. Whittall returned from General Course.	ShB

H.J. Gordon Dean Major
Commanding 7/L Lincs Regt.

Army Form C. 2118.

WAR DIARY
or
INTELLIGENCE SUMMARY.
(Erase heading not required.)

Instructions regarding War Diaries and Intelligence Summaries are contained in F.S. Regs., Part II. and the Staff Manual respectively. Title pages will be prepared in manuscript.

Hour, Date, Place	Summary of Events and Information	Remarks and references to Appendices
		FRANCE, BELGIUM, HAZEBROUCK 5a 1/100000
WINNEZEELE 19.9.'17	Individual training. Tactical exercise circles Company Commanders during g evening. Men's clothing ironed.	SAB
WINNEZEELE 20.9.'17 WATOU	Battn left Camp at 4.50am and marched via STEENVORDE, ABEEL to new Camp in WATOU area	SAB
WATOU 21.9.'17	Individual training. Night operations - exercise in laying tapes by Company for assembling troops for the attack.	SAB
22.9.'17	Individual training. 2nd Lt. J.H. Sutherland attached to 177th L.T.M.B.	SAB
WATOU } YPRES } 23.9.'17	Battn left Camp WATOU No 1 area at 9 am and proceeded to GOLDFISH CHATEAU, 1 mile W of YPRES on the YPRES - VLAMERTINGHE Rd, by route march and 15 mins.	SAB
YPRES 24.9.'17	Battn went into camp Reserve 11 inches near WIELTJE. A working party of B & D Coys were employed in the forward area. Transport and Specialists left our	SAB
25.9.'17	Battn moved to YORK Camp of attack moved nearer to front line and at mig ht formed up for attack	SAB
26.9.'17	Battn attacked at 5.50am on a 250 yds frontage. Capt. E.W. Hall was killed and the following officers wounded Lt Col A.B. Johnson, Capt A.G. Hooper, Capt G.D. Fox.	SAB Operation Order No. ❶ see appendices Nos 2, 3 + 4

H/Gordon Daaryin Lr
Commanding 14 Lines Regt.

WAR DIARY or **INTELLIGENCE SUMMARY.**

Army Form C. 2118.

(Erase heading not required.)

Hour, Date, Place	Summary of Events and Information	Remarks and references to Appendices
		FRANCE & BELGIUM.
YPRES. 26.9.17 continued.	Capt E.V.G. KNOX Capt M.J.M. GALE 2Lt. H.R. SMITH 2nd Lt.I.R. SCOTT Lt.T.R. COULSON 2nd Lt.G. HILLARY and Lt E.W. BARKER further ranks 36 killed 144 wounded 18 missing. The attack was successful. Battn was relieved in the front line by the 2/4 Lincolnshire Regt. and went into support.	HAZEBROUCK 5.a. 11/00000 Les essarties N°25
27.9.17	Battn in support - to the two front line Battns.	SMS
28.9.17	Battn were relieved on night to by the 1st CANTERBURY	G.B. SMS
29.9.17	Regt. N.Z. Expeditionary Force. 2nd Lt F.C. ROBERTSON went on transport course. After relief Battn proceeded to RED ROSE CAMP, VLAMERTINGHE and arrived there at 12.30 am on the morning of the 30th inst. After arrival at Camp 1 man was killed and 1 man wounded together with 3 horses killed and 1 wounded by an aeroplane bomb dropped in the YPRES-POPERINGHE RD near BRANDHOEK.	SMS
VLAMERTINGHE 30.9.17 WATOU	Battn moved by motor lorries to FORTH Camp WATOU N° 1 area. Major H.G. DEAN returned from course and took over command of Battn.	SMS

H.G.on Dean Major
Commanding 2/4 Lincs Regt.

2/4th LINCOLNSHIRE REGT.
OPERATION ORDER No. 19.

SECRET   COPY No.

Barrage map attached   14th September
Scale 1/10000

1. The enemy are known to be holding four concrete strong points as shown on barrage map, each with about 40 men & 1 machine gun.

2. The 177th Infantry will attack and consolidate the position shown approximately by the line A.-B. The 176th Infantry Bde will be on the right, and the Y.Z. Infantry Bde on the left.
   Boundary lines are shown on the attached map.

3. The attack will be carried out by the 2/4th Leicester Regt: supported by the 2/4th Lincoln Regt: After the capture of the 1st objective — shown on barrage map by the line C-D — the 2/4th Lincoln Regt: will pass through the Bn in front, and capture and consolidate the line A.-B. (2nd objective), occupying any captured strong points.

4. The Bn will attack with A & D Companies in front line A. on the right D on the left. B Company will be in support 70x in rear of the leading companies. C. Company will be in reserve & will follow up 100x behind the support Company. Each Company will attack on a 2 platoon frontage.

5. Bn H.Q. will be at K.31.c.9.5. until the 2nd objective is captured when it will move to strong point K.38.a.1.8.

6. Two Vickers guns are attached to the Bn and will move forward with the support Company.

7. The S.O. will arrange visual signalling with A.D. & B. Companies and Bde H.Q. after capture of 2nd objective.

8. Barrage time table will be as shown on barrage map attached.

9. Watches will be synchronised at Bn H.Q at 8.45 a.m.

10. Dress:— Fighting Order.

11. Zero will be at 9.30 am 15th

12. 50 men of the 2/4th Leicesters will carry S.A.A. etc for the Bn

2.

13. The most advanced troops will be prepared to light flares when they are called for by contact aeroplane

Issued by cyclist orderly at 3 p.m.

Copy No 1. 177th Infantry Brigade
       2 A. Company
       3 B   "
       4 C   "
       5 D   "
       6 I.O.
       7 Signals
       8 Transport
       9 4th Leicesters
     10 M.G.Coy..

Capt & Adjt
2/5 Lincoln Regt:

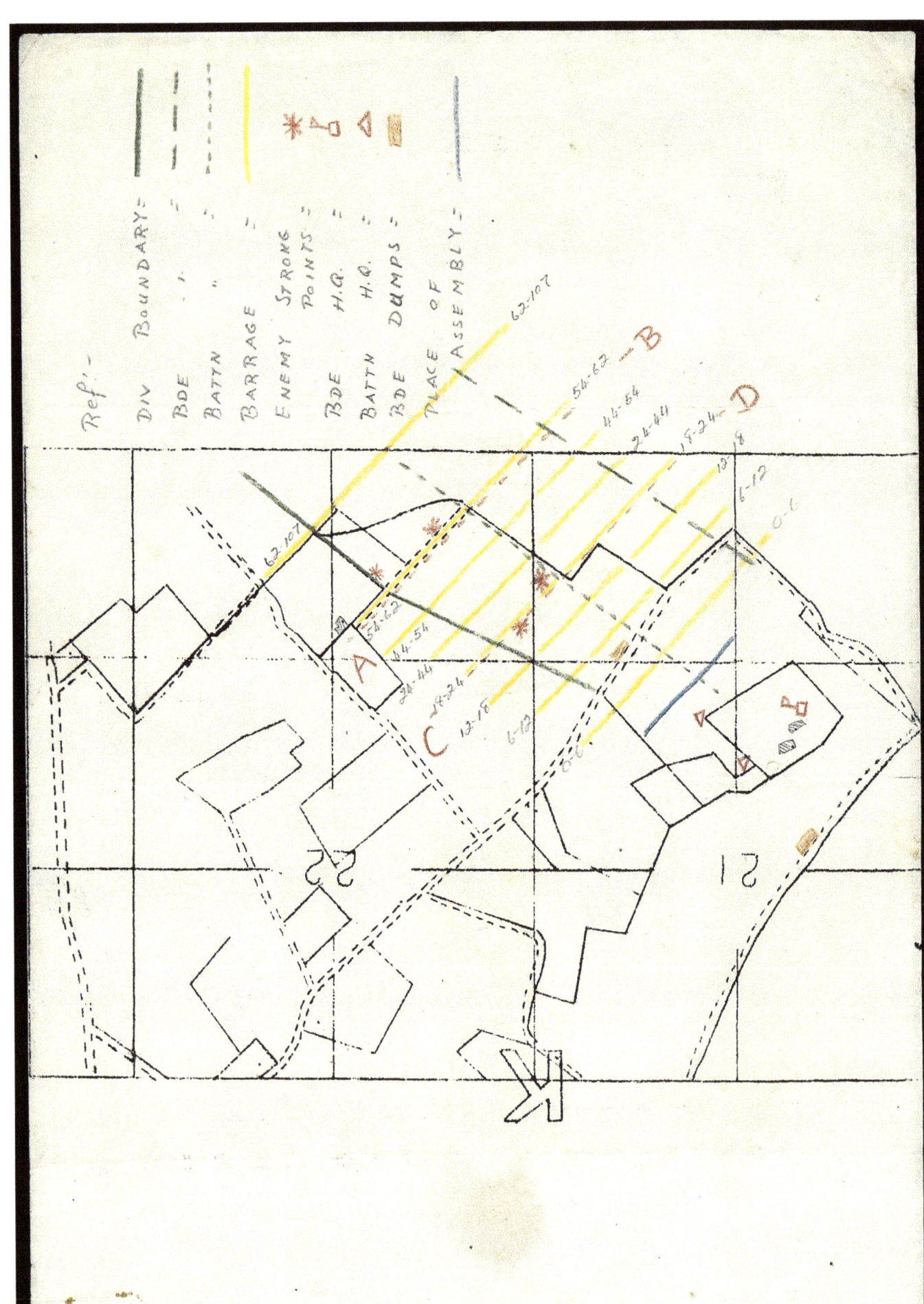

ORIGINAL

CONFIDENTIAL

Army Form C. 2118.

WAR DIARY
or
INTELLIGENCE SUMMARY.
(Erase heading not required.)

Instructions regarding War Diaries and Intelligence Summaries are contained in F.S. Regs., Part II. and the Staff Manual respectively. Title pages will be prepared in manuscript.

3/W/WOOD.N.F.

OCTOBER 1917.

Hour, Date, Place	Summary of Events and Information	Remarks and references to Appendices
WATOU. 1.10.17	2L Battn. arrived at FORTH CAMP on the night of 30th Sept/1st October. The FORTH Camp was in occupation of M.G. Batty of New Zealanders and in consequence the Battn. bivouaced in a field adjoining.	FRANCE & BELGIUM HAZEBROUCK S/2 1/100000
WATOU 2.10.17 ST VENANT	Battn. marched at 7 am to rail area. by motor lorries. Arrived at dining at noon. Bistro SGHS - 3 miles W of ST VENANT on the ST VENANT - GUARBECQUE Road.	S.43
ST VENANT 3.10.17	One hour Physical Training, Musketry, Squad drill & Clothing Capt. Simpson (R.A.M.C.) rejoined to Battn & duty. Arrival young by O.C. St Albans & the Officers of the 26 Septs. on which he congratulated the Battn on its success.	S.43
" 4.10.17	Physical training as for 3rd Inst. 6 Officer and 35 O Ranks rejoined from Australian Depot. The names of the officers are Lt. C.C.H.GREAVES, 2Lt. P.E.COTTIS, 2Lt G.P.READER 2L.S.W.MACKENZIE W.G. ALLEN, 2L. W.J. WODLHEADS. Coy Parades at 9.10 am for training.	S.43
" 5.10.17	Battn moved to BOXY area. by route march and motor lorries.	S.43
VENANT }6.10.17 ORNY ST JULIEN}	A & D Coys left at 7 am and marched to point GE8820 and awaited arrival of motor lorries conveying B & C Coys. B & C Coys turned out 9 am and arrived at point GE8820 at 10.30 am & the A & D Coys embussed. Art Coys then proceeded by route march to ORNY ST JULIEN. The day was very cold and wet	S.43

J. Porter Dean
Lt Col
Commanding 3L Lines NF

WAR DIARY
or
INTELLIGENCE SUMMARY

Army Form C. 2118.

October 1917.

Place	Date	Hour	Summary of Events and Information	Remarks and references to Appendices
				FRANCE
Y ST JULIEN	7-10-17		Winters kit came into possession at 1pm. Batn 16 March parade at 10.45am. Arty demonstration at 11.45am.	HAZEBROUCK AREA M100040
"	8.10.17		Company and Individual training.	B3.
"	9.10.17		Company and Individual training. Received orders to move 15 miles nearby by 177th Div. Order ref. move cancelled.	B3.
Y ST JULIEN STROS	10.10.17		Batn attached to 178th Bde and march orders received by G.O.C. 178th Inf. Bde to HESTRUD. LENS. 11 The Weather was very bad. The march commenced at 10am. Batn was allowed 15 min en route. The Batn arrived at its destination at 2.30pm.	1 D95 40
STROS OIEVAL	11.10.17		The Batn moved by route march to OIEVAL - P.F. 40.20. March commenced at 9.45am and the Batn arrived at OIEVAL at 12 noon.	BB SAS.
OIEVAL AIN	12.10.17		The Batn marched to OHLAIN (LENS II) (I.H.II.) Billets were found for the night. The 2nd Bn's were along the S side of the Bois de HAZOIS. 18.94.5.19.04. were found to be almost impassable and is nothing more than a track.	BB
AIN AREA HEZ AREA FIVE VALLEY	13.10.17		The 177th Bde relieved the 3rd Canadian Inf Bde in the AVION sector and the Batn went into Bde reserve [VIMY 36.c.SW3] S14 at ZOUAVE Valley to 5/14 the Bde night was spent in dug-outs and shelters in BLUEBELL Camp. The weather continues very bad.	MB
HEZ AREA BELL CAMP	14.10.17		At 2pm Coy hd Bde. moved into NEBERTH camp. Returned on H.L. SOUCHEZ - CARENCY RD at (LENS. 11). Working parties were found. Parties consisting of 4 Officers + 300 O.Rs made for work in trenches of SIVENCHY 2.J.26 (LENS. II).	MB

A.D.S.S./Forms/C. 2118.

H.H. Gordon Major
Commanding 2/7 Manco Regt.

Army Form C. 2118.

WAR DIARY
or
INTELLIGENCE SUMMARY.
(Erase heading not required.)

Instructions regarding War Diaries and Intelligence Summaries are contained in F.S. Regs., Part II CONFIDENTIAL and the Staff Manual respectively. Title pages will be prepared in manuscript.

Place	Date	Hour	Summary of Events and Information	Remarks and references to Appendices
				FRANCE LENS
RENCY AREA.	15.10.17		A working party consisting of 1 Officer & 35 O.Rs for work on TOTTENHAM CAMP SOUCHEZ. The night working parties consisting of 6 Officers and 300 other Ranks in charge of Capt Wilmshurst for work in forward area left at 6 p.m. The others returns by Lawrence's section.	A.B.
			Of 1 O.R. wounded.	
	16.10.17		Company Commanders went into forward area to reconnoitre and arrange details for relief to take place on night of 17/18th Oct. Working party of 1 Officer & 20 O.Rs continued work at TOTTENHAM CAMP. Night working parties as per previous diary.	(1) Relief orders
RENCY COULOTTE	17.10.17		The Battn started. Relief orders issued. The Battn went into the front line in the AVION Sector relieving 2/5th Leicesters. Reports from the relief BR Battn without a hitch and was completed in excellent time. Reports all Companies in Reports at 10.25 p.m.	SHEET 36C S.W.
			Both Coys were activity at #T.1 a 69 (Sheet 36 C S.W)	A.B.
	18.10.17		Patrols sent out from left front line at N36d34 but no movement of enemy reported. Gas projected for the night consisting only of unfavourable conditions. Artillery went over at 7 o'clock on the evening from N36.b.64. No reference during Line unable to get in touch with enemy. Weather fine. Conditions normal.	
	19.10.17		Patrol went over at N36.b.34. No information secured. No Man's Land was practically all flooded in front of the front line and movement was confined to a small area. Gas projected from front line. Situation normal. Artillery activity on right & on left. No movement of front line or forward. Enemy movements cept of Returned time went canopying.	A.B.

H. Gordon Dron
Major
Commanding 2/4 Lincs Regt.

Army Form C. 2118.

WAR DIARY
or
INTELLIGENCE SUMMARY.
(Erase heading not required.)

Place	Date	Hour	Summary of Events and Information	Remarks and references to Appendices
CULOTTE	20.10.17		Patrols as for yesterday. Situation normal. Gas projectors connected at last moment owing to unfavourable conditions. Weather fine. During the day an aerial fight took place over our lines in which one old	FRANCE SHEET 36 S.W.
"	21.10.17		aeroplane and artillery plane put to flight 3 enemy planes, forcing one to come within the enemy lines. A/Capt A.P.O. WARD went on leave. Orders issued for relief. Owing to breakdown of railway relieving battalion 2/6th S.Staffs who were	NB Divisional orders 26 — (2) PB
"	22.10.17		to relieve at 7pm did not arrive until 2 am on morning of 23.10.17. 2/Lt ONSTON WORMALD	SHEET 36 B.S.W.
CHÂTEAU DE LA HAIE			Relief reported completed at 3am. The Battn was conveyed to CHATEAU de la HAIE W/D central by lorries. Light railway arriving at destination at 7am. 2/Lts. HILLERY, REVILL, JOHNSON reported for duty from HQ full Base. Carrying party of 1 NCO + 35 ORs to SOUCHEZ to road party from 178th Inf.Bde. GB	VANCOUVER CAMP
"	23.10.17		Specialist classes arranged. Working parties were sent for Base Transport lines., R.E. Squads, Town Major at SOUCHEZ at 6pm. The following officers reported for duty. 2/Lts. TOLSON, SMIRLEY, PILGRIM, LIPSHBROOKE, and VINCENT.	PB
"	24.10 17		2nd Lt ONSTON appointed chief of normad. Specialist training. Working parties as for previous day. Following officers reported for duty 2/Lts ASH PATTERSON, L.E. WHARTON, J.COX, S.R.SLIDEL, + J.G. PIPPET.	B
"	25.10 17		Specialist training. Working parties. Scheme for proper drainage of VANCOUVER CAMP commenced. 2/Lt Andrews proceeded to England on leave. 2/Lt THAIN + 2/Lt SQUIRREL returned from leave.	AB

L/Gordon Major
Commanding 2/4 Batt Lincs Regt

WAR DIARY or INTELLIGENCE SUMMARY

Army Form C. 2118.

(Erase heading not required.)

Place	Date	Hour	Summary of Events and Information	Remarks and references to Appendices
				SHEET 36 B SW.
E.	26.10.17		Showered morning. Working parties as for yesterday. G.O.C Division visited VANCOUVER CAMP	9B.
	27.10.17		Showered. Training working parties as for yesterday. Church	9B.
	28.10.17		Working parties as for yesterday. Battn. Parade at Chateau de la Haie.	9B.
	29.10.17		Preparing to move. VANCOUVER CAMP handed over to 2/6 th N STAFFS. Battn entrained at 6 p.m arrived at RED MILL SIDING, LIEVIN at 8.45. Relief of 2/5 N STAFFS in support in LIEVIN effected and reported. 6	Operation order No 27-(3) SHEET. LENS 36 c SW.1.
LIEVIN			Brigade at 10 pm. Gas guards consisting of 1 NCO + 9 men mounted at Red Hugo, Battn HdQrs M23 c 33	9B.
	30.10.17		Working parties found for work in forward areas, Full Battn Strength	9B.
	31.10.17		Same working parties as for yesterday. In proportion of gas masks made from Divt front.	9B.

H Gordon Drew
Major Commanding 2/4 Lincs Regt.

ORIGINAL

WAR DIARY
2/4 LINCOLN REGT
INTELLIGENCE SUMMARY
NOVEMBER 1917
Vol 10

Army Form C. 2118.
CONFIDENTIAL
177/59

Place	Date	Hour	Summary of Events and Information	Remarks and references to Appendices
LIEVIN. S SECTOR	1st Nov 17.		Working parties – Full Batn strength. The honours won by the Batn during the operation of the 26th Sept 1917 in the YPRES salient were published today. 24.7/c Ransom RFA made prisoner.	FRANCE. LENS. 36cSW1. I SHB
"	2.	11.17	Working parties as for yesterday.	SHB
"	3.	11.17	Working parties as for yesterday. Capt A.P.O.HARD rejoined from leave	SHB
"	4.	11.17	Working parties as for yesterday. 2Lt Revie & 8 others became casualties from gas poisoning	SHB
"	5.	11.17	Working parties as for yesterday	SHB
"	6.11.17.		The Battn relieved the 2/5th Battn Leicestershire Regt in front line. A Coy in the Left. N3d M3u65u M3b6a Support Lt B.un Newnum. & Batton H.Qrs at M23 d 37.	Operation No 28 Op. Orders No 2.
"	7.	11.17	D Coy on Right. C Coy in the Support. 2nd Lt H.P. BARKER joined from leave. LIEUT R.J.M.ANDREWS rejoined from leave.	SHB
"	8.	11.17	Situation normal. "	SHB
"	9.	11.17	Situation normal. 2 men wounded	SHB
"	10.	11.17	4 men wounded. A flying patrol consisting of an officer 2Lt G.P.Reddish, 1NCO + 2 other ranks went out from left front by in order to get in contact with enemy. No enemy were encountered. Two flares were sent out from R front lay. 1st consisting of an officer, 2Lt LATHAROOKE and a NCO + 2 men reconnoitred the LENS-ARRAS road in the vicinity of N20 a 25.50. Negative information rep obtained. 2nd consisting of 1 NCO + 2 men reconnoitred the junction of the communication 2/4 Lincoln Regt.	App. 3

T.R.Vnief Major
Comm'ing 2/4 Lincoln Regt

Army Form C. 2118.

WAR DIARY
or
INTELLIGENCE SUMMARY.

(Erase heading not required.)

Confidential

Instructions regarding War Diaries and Intelligence Summaries are contained in F.S. Regs., Part II. and the Staff Manual respectively. Title pages will be prepared in manuscript.

Place	Date	Hour	Summary of Events and Information	Remarks and references to Appendices
LENS	10/11/17	Cont'd.	LIEVIN – LENS + LENS – ARRAS Road. No enemy encountered. Capt J. Hanley to hospital	LENS. 36C S.W.I. SB
"	11/11/17		Inter-company relief. 2nd Lt J.E. Rogers went on Course. 1st Army. 2nd Lt E.R. Beecroft joined from Base	SB Operation Order Appx 4
"	12/11/17		Situation normal.	SB
"	13/11/17		" Capt B.H. Challinor reported for duty.	SB Operation Order Appx 5
LIEVIN	14/11/17		Battn relieved by "C" Canadian Battn. Companies proceeded independently to ALBERTA CAMP. SOUCHEZ	SB S.E. Appx 7
Camp Souchez	15/11/17		Battn. Battn moved at 2.30 pm to GOUY SERVINS. Accidental death of 30397 Pte Stuart	36 C S.E. Operation Order No 30. Appx.
"	16/11/17		Specialist training and open warfare. Capt R.B. Whitworth evacuated to hospital. Capt J. Service (RAMC) took in SB.	SB
HABARCQ	17/11/17		Battn moved by route march to HABARCQ	SB Operation Order No 31. Appx 7
"	18/11/17		Church Parade. 2Lt G. Tilson, 2nd Lt N.J. Hopkins & 2nd Lt R.E. Atherton proceeded on Course to II Corps School	SB Operation Order No 32 Appx. 8
BAILLEULMONT	19/11/17		Battn march at 4.30 pm by route march to BAILLEULMONT. Major Ward returned from leave.	SB
"	20/11/17		Lectures to Platoons by Platoon Commanders on Open Warfare. 2Lt T.C. Robinson proceeded on leave	SB
ACHIET-LE-PETIT	21/11/17		Moved by route march to ACHIET-LE-PETIT. G.114 & (37c) 2nd Lt W. Parkes and wounded to hospital	SB Operation Order No 33. Appx. 9
"	22/11/17		Cleaning up.	SB
"	23/11/17		Marched to ACHIET LE GRAND, entrained to FINS, marched to camp in BERTRAM WOOD.	SB Operation Order No 34 Appx. 10
(BERTRAM WOOD)	24/11/17		Major T.H.S. Granath took command of Battn. 2Lt D.F. Nickolls reported to hospital sick. 1 Offr & 25 ORs	SB Something heavily from working party returned
"	25/11/17		Church parade. Working party consisting of 1 offr & 25 ORs	SB

Signed T.H.S. Granath Major
Commanding 2/4 Batt Lincoln L.I. Regt

Army Form C. 2118.

WAR DIARY
or
INTELLIGENCE SUMMARY.
(Erase heading not required.)

Instructions regarding War Diaries and Intelligence Summaries are contained in F. S. Regs., Part II. and the Staff Manual respectively. Title pages will be prepared in manuscript.

Place	Date	Hour	Summary of Events and Information	Remarks and references to Appendices
FINS.	26/11/17		Austin Battn. 2Lt G.R.Parry proceeded on course F. III Corps school.	France SH 57 c.
"			Training carried out through during week. Battn. moved to bivouacs at Ref Q 15 b for night.	58
RESCAULT	27.11.17			SH 8"
RESCAULT- FLESQUIRES	28.11.17		Battn. moves to FLESQUIRES and established Hd.quarters at R 13 d 95. 3 other Companies proceeded in manner to III Corps scheme	58
FLESQUIRES	29.11.17		In FLESQUIRES. 2nd Lt Stilling attached as Town Major FLESQUIRES.	88 "
"	30.11.17		Heavy enemy counter attacks to N.W. and S. Enemy reported broken through at about Q 30 + 36 R 25 + 31. Reported capture of village of FLESQUIRES commenced. 3 Corps H.Q. at Q 13 round N. corner of village. 4 May "C" Coy took up defensive position in trench Q 17 b. "Great artillery and aerial activity."	88 "

T.H. Howard Major
Commanding 1/4 Bn Lincolnshire Regt.

CONFIDENTIAL

WAR DIARY
2/4 LINCOLN REGT. Original
INTELLIGENCE SUMMARY.

(Erase heading not required.)

Army Form C. 2118.

DECEMBER 1917.

Place	Date	Hour	Summary of Events and Information	Remarks and references to Appendices
FLESQUIÈRES	1/12/17		French scheme for the defence of the village of FLESQUIÈRES continued. During the afternoon "Brand 16" was mined. At 5:30pm the all clear was received and the Bn stood down. There was minor artillery activity on both flanks which increased to great violence in the direction of MOEUVRES. 2/Lt O.F.NICHOLLS returned from hospital. A/Capt A.P.O.WARD and 2/Lt ALLEN were attached to 2/5 Lincoln Regt.	FRANCE 57c.
				SHS
FLESQUIÈRES BOURLON WOOD	2/12/17		The Bn moved into support in BOURLON WOOD occupying the line vacated by 2/4 Lincoln Regt. Two companies "C" & "D" men in close support in F.19.b and two companies A & B sup " in SUNKEN ROAD (?/c) Bn Hdqrs here established in S.W. corner of BOURLON Wood at F.13.c.81	AB
BOURLON WOOD	3/12/17		On the evening of this day the Bn relieved the 2/4th Leicester Regt in the front line in BOURLON Wood occupying a line of posts running from F.5.6.4.5, G.F.4.4.2 & B.6.1 & D boop wes in front and A by in close support about F.13.6.4.1. During the night the wood was heavily bombarded with gas shells from which the Bn suffered no casualties. A day of forward artillery company tactics for front line boys. Casualties 1 other rank wounded. 2 ½5 Lincoln Regt, ¼ ulans from Curzee T Cop's & the Fusrs Rhodes Woodlands replied from ? Corps school.	BD

Commg 2/4 Bn Lincolnshire Regt.

WAR DIARY
INTELLIGENCE SUMMARY.

Army Form C. 2118.

Confidential (Erase heading not required.) Original.

Place	Date	Hour	Summary of Events and Information	Remarks and references to Appendices
BOURLON WOOD	4/12/17		During the day the C.O. was summoned to attend a conference at Brigade H.Qrs. Later orders were received to prepare to evacuate the wood. Capt K. Howes took charge of the operations in the wood. All regimental stores etc. were collected and sent down narrow gauge of artillery. The evacuation was carried out with precision. One platoon of 'B' Coy under the command of 2/Lt Ruffell acted as rearguard and remained in wood until 3.30 am on morning of 5th. After evacuation A + B Coys dug in along line Sunken Rd (noted) Major H.G. Doan took command of these Coys. C + D Coys occupied trenches in the Hindenburg Support line at K 24 + 34. There were no casualties during the evacuation. Bn HQrs established at K 24 a 34.	FRANCE 57 C
FLESQUIÈRES	5/12/17		Remainder of the line L.I.R. completed. Small posts and a front were wired with apron wire. The position was shelled at intervals. The trenches required by C + D Coys in the Hindenburg Support line were shelled intermittently during the day. Reorganisation of defence was carried out. Bn headqrs was bombed by E.A. Several casualties inflammable results not	
	6/12/17		Owing to the withdrawal of the 6th Bde on our right 'B' Coy dug a defensive flank facing S.E. Immediately this was completed 'B' Coy withdrew to the Hindenburg Support line at dusk having the fight during the Jun Huruk.	

T.H. Enraght
Comdg. 2/th Bn Lincolnshire Regt

CONFIDENTIAL

Army Form C. 2118.

WAR DIARY
INTELLIGENCE SUMMARY.
(Erase heading not required.)

Original

Instructions regarding War Diaries and Intelligence Summaries are contained in F. S. Regs., Part II. and the Staff Manual respectively. Title pages will be prepared in manuscript.

Place	Date	Hour	Summary of Events and Information	Remarks and references to Appendices
	6/12/17 continued		During the morning many small parties of the enemy were seen moving in the direction of ANNEUX and GRAINCOURT. At 3pm the enemy launched an attack on outpost line, which was successful (Appendix I)	FRANCE 57 C.
	7/12/17		The situation was normal. Reorganisation of Bn in Hindenburg support line took place. Consolidating the line was continued. 3rd W. Yorks were was relieved by 5th N. Staffs Regt.	AB
	8.12.17		Working parties & loops were employed on Hindenburg defences	AB
	9.12.17		" "	AB
TRESCAULT	10.12.17		The Bn was relieved by the 2/5th N. Staffs Regt. and retired to old Bruised front line at [illegible]	AB
TRESCAULT	11.12.17		The Bn was employed on deepening the old Hindenburg line continuously in 1835 F3	AB
	12.12.17		Do for yesterday	AB
	13.12.17		Do for yesterday	AB
	14.12.17		The work of deepening the Hindenburg line continued. 12 noon. During the afternoon the area was taken over by the 3/5th Bn Lincolnshire Regt. and the Bn proceeded to	
LECHELLE				AB

T. M. [illegible] Lt Col.
Comm'g 2/4 Berkshire Regt.

CONFIDENTIAL.

Army Form C. 2118.

WAR DIARY
or
INTELLIGENCE SUMMARY.

Original.

(Erase heading not required.)

Instructions regarding War Diaries and Intelligence Summaries are contained in F. S. Regs., Part II. and the Staff Manual respectively. Title pages will be prepared in manuscript.

Place	Date	Hour	Summary of Events and Information	Remarks and references to Appendices
LECHELLE	15.12.17		The day was devoted to cleaning up and baths	FRANCE AB 57d
BERTINCOURT	16.12.17		The Bn moved to Bertincourt. 2/4th Lincolnshire proceeded on leave.	AB
BERTINCOURT HAVRINCOURT	17.12.17		Five officers and 5 N.C.Os reconnoitred the left front line FLESQUIERES. Major Bevan went in charge of party.	
			Proceeded 15 ORs British front line in K.32.c.2.o to take over from 2/5 Lincoln Regt front line 18/12/15.	
			Went in a battalion parade for the presentation of ribbons and awards in connection with the action of the 26th Sept (Passchendaele Ridge) The following were presented with ribbons 2/Lt Joynes M.C. 2/Lt Squirrell M.C. Sgt F Bryant M.M. Cpl McDermott M.M. Pte Thompson M.O.1. Pte Smith G.E. M.M. Loads were distributed to Pte McBean Cpl Hislop Pte Gartshire	
			At 12.30pm the Bn moved to new area in K.33.c.2.o. The old British front line before Havrincourt. The day was very cold. Snow fell intermittently	SB.
FLESQUIERES	18/12/17		The Bn relieved the 2/5 S. Staffs in the left front line FLESQUIERES in K.18 a, b & D. Coys in front and supports in close support. Relief complete at 7.15pm Bn H.Qrs established at K.18.c.7.4. Working parties from support Coys worked on front wire	AB
"	19.12.17		Intermittent shelling of area. A fighting patrol consisting of 1 officer (2/Lt Batten) and 1 Sgt 12 ORs were left at 7pm and reconnoitred front K.7.13.c and limits of Zone A. No enemy were encountered.	

T H [Holmes?] Lt Col
Commanding 2/4 Bn Lincolnshire Regt.

CONFIDENTIAL

Army Form C. 2118.

WAR DIARY
or
INTELLIGENCE SUMMARY.
(Erase heading not required.)

Original.

Instructions regarding War Diaries and Intelligence Summaries are contained in F.S. Regs., Part II. and the Staff Manual respectively. Title pages will be prepared in manuscript.

Place	Date	Hour	Summary of Events and Information	Remarks and references to Appendices
ESQUIRES	19.12.17	Contd.	Another patrol left at 1 a.m. but found no sign of enemy occupation. All available men from support Coys worked in front line.	FRANCE 57.c a3.
	20.12.17		The situation was normal. Occasional shelling. The front was locally and its artillery were informed. All available men from two support Coys were employed wiring the front. Several encounters.	
			No enemy encountered. An enemy wiring party was located and its artillery were informed. All available men from two support Coys were employed wiring the front. Several encounters	
			resulted during the day. The weather was intensely cold and wintry. Capt. G.D. Fox reported as adjutant	13
	21.12.17		Situation normal. Patrols and wiring parties as for yesterday.	W5
	22.12.17		The Bn was relieved by the 10th Lancashire Fusiliers & Bn went into & TRESCAULT and	
			Kept up the area vacated by the relieving Bn.	
	23.12.17		The Bn marched to rest billets at ROCQUIGNY.	
			Capt. G.R. Sherwell, Capt. E. Elliott, 2nd Lieut G.E. Elliott, 2nd Lieut W.S. Page and 20 O.R. arrived as reinforcements.	
ROCQUIGNY	24.12.17		Lieut W.S. Payne and 2nd Lieut J.E. Rogers proceeded to England on leave.	G.R.F.
	25.12.17		The Battalion marched to BAPAUME and travelled by troop train to TINQUES, thence by	G.R.F.
			march route to MAIZIERES, where the Battalion went into billets.	
	26.12.17		Rev. H.A.N. Tronton C.F. reported for duty as chaplain	G.R.F.

T M Sherwell Lt Col

Comm'g: 2/4 Lin as Regt.

CONFIDENTIAL.

Army Form C. 2118.

WAR DIARY
INTELLIGENCE SUMMARY.

(Erase heading not required.)

Original

Instructions regarding War Diaries and Intelligence Summaries are contained in F. S. Regs., Part II. and the Staff Manual respectively. Title pages will be prepared in manuscript.

Place	Date	Hour	Summary of Events and Information	Remarks and references to Appendices
MAIZIERES	27.12.17		Training.	FRANCE CAN (RENS !!) ON STG.Idii
"	28.12.17		Capt. K.F. Howes proceeded to England for a course at Hythe Musketry School. Training	G.S.F.
"	29.12.17		Training continued. 2nd Lieut W.H. Patterson reported for duty from hospital.	G.S.F.
"	30.12.17		Church Parade. Christmas celebrations.	
"	31.12.17		Training.	

T.H. Johnson Lt Col.
Comdg 2/4 Bn Lincolnshire Regt.

To O.C.
2/4 LINCOLNS.

Report on Withdrawal of Rearguard, 177th Brigade.

Ref. Map - MOEUVRES Special Sheet
57c. Part 5.   7-12-17

SITUATION — On Dec. 4th at 11 p.m. 4/5th, I took command of "A" & "B" Companies (less 1 platoon) 2/4 LINCS REGT, under Lieut. Col. Marden D.S.O., 2/7th Sherwood Foresters, with orders to form part of a line for temporary defence on LA JUSTICE - GRAINCOURT Road. A line of two companies L.1 & L.3.7 to 100 yards East of LA JUSTICE - FLESQUIERES track. 14 posts were dug — 8 North and 6 South of LA JUSTICE - GRAINCOURT Road. The whole of the front was wired with apron fence. At 5.30 a.m. 5th, Lieut. of "A" Reppel and 1 platoon reported from BOURLON wood were taken they had acted as rearguard to the Battalion. This operation entailed hard work from 11 p.m. 4th to 7.15 a.m. 5th, from which time no movement was allowed by day. The weather was fine and very cold. Slight shelling during the afternoon of the 5th.

PATROL — At dusk a protective patrol of 1 N.C.O. & 4 men, was sent out to observe LA JUSTICE - ANNEUX Road junction during double wiring of whole front. Nothing to report. An enemy patrol (1 N.C.O. & 10 other ranks) surrounded LA JUSTICE buildings and searched them on instructions from O.C. Rearguard Coy. at 12 midnight 5/6th. No enemy were found.

PRISONERS — At 1.30 a.m. 6th, 3 men of an enemy patrol strayed near our wire and were killed and captured.

NEW POSITION ORDERS — At 3.30 a.m. 6th I was ordered to take up a new position during the withdrawal to be completed by 5 a.m. This entailed a movement half right and posts to be dug to accommodate one company. "B" Company was immediately given points on which to dig slit trenches, "A" Company holding all previous posts during the operation. The position (line Q.1 to L.7 U.23, inclusive) being dug, "B" Company took over posts from "A" Company, leaving 6 men to cover withdrawal. The covering party fired on enemy approaching mine, North of LA JUSTICE - GRAINCOURT Road. The withdrawal was complete by 5 a.m. 6th. My H.Q. L.7.85. "C" Company was ordered to withdraw immediately to Q La La.

ENEMY PATROLS — Morning of 6th very quiet. About 8 a.m. enemy reconnoitring patrol appeared at L.2. Cuirbel lying they were out of view about 300 yards in front of our position. This reported. In all 5 enemy patrols were reported on the left flank and instructions were asked for in case of attack.

AEROPLANE RECONNAISSANCE — Enemy aircraft low and very active in dropping signals.

WITHDRAWAL ORDERS. About 1.30 p.m. orders were received to withdraw in case of enemy attacking in force, otherwise no withdrawal would take place before dark. From 1.30 to about 3 p.m. the position was bombarded with H.E., a few casualties being caused.

WITHDRAWAL. About 3 p.m. enemy appeared in force and were reported in great strength on left flank. His bank had to withdraw to escape being encircled. I ordered "A" Company to conform. The withdrawal was carried out in very fair order all along the line.

ACTION. The enemy advanced close to ORIVAL WOOD from the right front about 200 arriving on East side of wood at the same moment when 4/4 LINCS and H.Q. were withdrawing through the wood. Enemy were heavily fired on at close quarters and several casualties inflicted. "A" Company and H.Q. withdrew to western edge of wood and got clear. The enemy fired from the hip continuously and several men were wounded - 2/Lt. Johnson being wounded twice in foot and arm. A general halt was made on line of disused gun-pits for reforming, and enemy were heavily fired on but continued advancing. The withdrawal was continued, half the company passing through gap in wire L.18.b.6.3 and half at L.13.a.6.1. The latter party under 2/Lt Bates, with the Sherwood Foresiers, engaged the enemy in hand to hand fighting, crossing him to retire. The enemy occupied the outer defences of GRAINCOURT. The enemy occupied the BEET FACTORY trenches but were driven out by a party of 4/4 LINCS and 2/5 LEIRS, the 4/4 LINCS taking 3 prisoners. A machine gun was also taken by the LEICESTER REGT. The enemy continued advancing and was engaged by rifle and machine gun fire from FLESQUIÈRES defences, considerable casualties being inflicted. The party entering L.18.b.6.3 had every assistance and cover by Lt.Col. C.H. Bryant, who was controlling their fire very effectively, put out of action a number of the enemy. The remainder finally withdrew.

REMARKS. Throughout the whole of the activity all ranks were exceptionally cool and attentive to orders, in spite of three days and two nights of the greatest discomfort and hard work. Our casualties were 6 killed, 8 wounded, 7 missing.

I wish especially to bring to your notice the conduct of the following :-

2/Lieut. P.E. COTTIS commanding "A" Coy, who behaved extremely well during the action keeping his men well in hand and displaying great personal courage. He counter-attacked the enemy who had occupied a small trench near the BEETROOT FACTORY, afterwards holding

No. 200933 Acting C.S.M. F. BRYANT, who organised the men near him in a fire position on gun pits (sketch map) whilst under heavy fire. Later he did very good work whilst in P.C. support defences.

2/Lieut. P.E. COTTIS reports No. 202015 P/c. W.E. Brown and No. 202663 Pte. J. Lanckier, who carried his orders to his N.C.O.'s repeatedly and with promptitude in spite of heavy enemy machine gun and rifle fire."

H. Gordon Drew
Major
2/4 Lincolnshire Regt.

7.12.17.

Original.

2/4th Lincolns

CONFIDENTIAL.   Army Form C. 2118.

WAR DIARY
or
INTELLIGENCE SUMMARY.
(Erase heading not required.)

JANUARY 1918

Ref. FRANCE SIC.E II. LENS II.

Instructions regarding War Diaries and Intelligence Summaries are contained in F. S. Regs., Part II. and the Staff Manual respectively. Title pages will be prepared in manuscript.

Place	Date	Hour	Summary of Events and Information	Remarks and references to Appendices
MAIZIERES	1.1.18		Lieut-Col. J.H.S. Swanton and 2nd Lieut H.E. Godfrey proceeded to England on 14 days leave. Major H.G. Dean assumed command of the Bn in absence of C.O. Capt H. Ward 2i/c in command. Training resumed	GSF
"	2.1.18		As for previous day. Capt. G.W. Border transferred to 'A' Coy. 2nd in command.	GSF
"	3.1.18		Brigade Tactical Exercise without troops. Lieut C. Blanzier rejoined from ?	GSF
"			59 Div. Reinforcement Camp. Training continued	GSF
"	4.1.18		" "	GSF
"	5.1.18		Divisional Tactical Exercise without troops. 2nd Lieut J.D.R. Gill.	GSF
"			and R.A. Pearce on leave to England	
"	6.1.18		Battalion Church Parade	GSF
"	7.1.18		Capt. R.B. Wilmhurst rejoined unit from sick leave in England and took command of 'B' Coy. Capt. E.E. Elliott transferred to 1/4th Lincolns. Training continued	GSF
"	8.1.18		Training continued	GSF
"	9.1.18		Brigade Adv. Guard Scheme without troops. Lieut H. Wright on leave to England.	GSF

Comm'g 2/4 Lincolns

34.K

Original

2/4 Lincolns
WAR DIARY
—OR—
INTELLIGENCE SUMMARY.

Army Form C. 2118.

CONFIDENTIAL.

(Erase heading not required.)

Instructions regarding War Diaries and Intelligence Summaries are contained in F. S. Regs., Part II and the Staff Manual respectively. Title pages will be prepared in manuscript.

Place	Date	Hour	Summary of Events and Information	Remarks and references to Appendices
				Ref. FRANCE 51C E&IE LEWS 11
MAIZIERES	10.1.18		Training continued. 2nd Lieut G.G. Hillery reported to A.T.M. for traffic duties. 2nd Lieut S. Payne and 2nd Lieut J.E. Rogers returned from leave.	G.S.F.
"	11.1.18		Battalion Inspection by G.O.C. Division. Major-General C.F. Romer C.B.,C.B. & g.,A.D.C. Arrival 53 O.R. re-inforcements. 2nd Lieut R. Pilgrim appointed Battalion Bombing Officer.	G.S.F.
"	12.1.18		Battalion Route march.	G.S.F.
"	13.1.18		Battalion Church Parade. 2nd Lieut H. Jeynes on 14 days leave to England.	G.S.F.
"	14.1.18		Training continued.	G.S.F.
"	15.1.18		"	G.S.F.
"	16.1.18		" Arrival of 32 O.R. re-inforcements.	G.S.F.
"	17.1.18		" Lieut-Col. J.H.S. Swanton returned from leave and re-assumed command of the Bn.	G.S.F.
"	18.1.18		" 2nd Lieut H.E. Godfrey returned from leave.	G.S.F.
"	19.1.18		Brigade Run. Course — MAZIERES — LIGNEREUIL — GIVENCHY — VILLERS-SIR-SIMON — PENIN — MAZIERES. Distance 8 miles. Only a small percentage completed the course within the time limit of 1hr. 20 mins.	G.S.F.

Commg. 2/4 Bn Lines Regt.

Original.

2/4th Lincolns

CONFIDENTIAL.

Army Form C. 2118.

WAR DIARY
or
INTELLIGENCE SUMMARY.
(Erase heading not required.)

Instructions regarding War Diaries and Intelligence Summaries are contained in F.S. Regs., Part II. and the Staff Manual respectively. Title pages will be prepared in manuscript.

Place	Date	Hour	Summary of Events and Information	Remarks and references to Appendices
MAIZIERES	26.1.18		Brigade Church Parade at AMBRINES. A card for gallantry presented by G.O.C. Division to Pte. J. Donskie 2/4 Lincolns. In the 1st round for the Divisional Football Challenge Cup the 2/4 Lincolns defeated the 2/5 Sherwoods by 1-0.	Ref. FRANCE 51c S.E.1 LENS 11. G.S.T.
"	21.1.18		Training continued. Instruction in the German Machine Gun by O.C. 200 M.G. Coy. Major H.G. Bean proceeded on 14 days leave to England. Capt. A. Ward attached H.Q. as 2 in Command.	G.S.T.
"	22.1.18		Training continued. 2nd Lieuts. T.D.R. Cully and R.A. Peacock returned from leave.	G.S.T.
"	23.1.18		Lieut-Col. T.H.S. Swanton acted as Brigadier in "	G.S.T.
"	24.1.18		Brigade Advanced Guard and Outpost scheme near PENIN. Training continued. 2/4 Lincolns defeated 2/4 Leicesters by 1-0 in the 2nd round of the Divisional Football Challenge Cup competition.	G.S.T.
"	25.1.18		Training continued.	G.S.T.
"	26.1.18		The Battalion proceeded by route march to LIENCOURT to witness Semi final round of Div. Football Challenge Cup. Result – D.A.C. 1 goal 2/4 Lincolns 0.	G.S.T.

Lieut. Col.
Comm'd'g. 2/4 Lincolns.

Original.

2/4 Lincolns.

CONFIDENTIAL   Army Form C. 2118.

WAR DIARY
INTELLIGENCE SUMMARY.

(Erase heading not required.)

Instructions regarding War Diaries and Intelligence
Summaries are contained in F. S. Regs., Part II.
and the Staff Manual respectively. Title pages
will be prepared in manuscript.

Place	Date	Hour	Summary of Events and Information	Remarks and references to Appendices
IZIERES	27.1.18		Battalion Church Parade.	Ref. FRANCE SIC E.I.I. LENS II. G/57.
"	28.1.18		Training continued	G/57.
"	29.1.18		2nd Lieut. H. Joyner returned from leave.	G/57.
"	30.1.18		Following Officers arrived from 1/4th Lincolns for amalgamation with 2/4th Lincolns. Lieut-Colonel G.A.Yool (to command amalgamated Battalion) Capt. R.N. Holmes (Adjutant). Capt. S. Lee, Capt. E.E. Elliott, Capt. A.E. Stephenson, Lieut & Q.M. T.W. Upex, 2nd Lieut. A.N. H. Bain, Capt. H.G. Ludoff. R.A.M.C.	G/57.
"	31.1.18		Re-organization of Battalion begun. The Battalion from the date of the amalgamation will be called the 4th Bn Lincolnshire Regt.	G/57.

T.H. Swan
Lieut-Colonel
Commanding 2/4 Lincolns.

OPERATION ORDERS No. 1

by Colonel A. Hutchinson. V.D.
Commanding 2/4 Bn. Lincs. Regt.

Reference ½" O.S. Sheet 29.   Luton. 22/6/15.

(1) **INFORMATION.**   The 2/1 N.M. Division will march to Easton Lodge, Great Dunmow, the fighting troops bivouacking there at 4 p.m. the 23rd. inst.

(2) **INTENTION.**   The column consisting of the 2/1 Lincoln & Leicester Brigade will march to-day, 22/6/15, to Ware via Dane End - Kimpton - Welwyn - Watton-at-Stone - and occupy billets as detailed by Brigade billeting party.

(3) **CONCENTRATION POINT.**   The Brigade will concentrate at the Cross Roads immediately S. of "F" in Dane End Farm at 9 a.m.

(4) **STORES.**   Companies will return to Store all Blankets in excess of 1 per Man at the following hours :-

     A   Company   6. 0 a.m.   C   Company   6.30 a.m.
     B   6.15 a.m.   D   6.45 a.m.

Kit Bags, containing surplus clothing, etc., will be stacked by Companies at the same hour in the yard adjoining the Q.M. Stores.

Ammunition at the rate of 120 rounds per Man will be drawn by Companies immediately and issued to Men on parade.

(5) **TRANSPORT.**   Transport will parade at 7.0 a.m. and Cooks Wagons will report at each Company Headquarters to load Cooking Utensils etc.

(6) **RETURNS.**   Report to reach this Office by 7 a.m. from each Company giving Nominal Roll of Men remaining behind for any reason. Sick etc. These Men to parade in front of Bn. Headquarters 1 hour after the departure of the Battalion. Companies will also at the same hour return to this Office their Billeting Books, Sheets, etc. together with cheques made payable to Lt. C.L. Harvey for the amount of billeting money due to date. Lt. C.L. Harvey will remain behind in charge of the Details and will be responsible for paying these, from the books and cheques left by the Companies, and will report when this has been completed to Headquarters at Ware, by Telegram. He will also re-billet together the Men left behind.

(7) **PARADE.**   Companies will parade at 8 a.m. and will move off 5 minutes later in the following order :- A. B. C. D. Dress - Field Service Marching Order each Man carrying in addition 1 Blanket, & 120 rounds of Ammunition. The Blanket is to be carried folded on top of the pack and the Waterproof Sheet round it so as to prevent it getting wet. He will also carry the current day's rations.

Issued to O.Sergts. as under :-
   A Coy.   7 Copies.   (Sgnd) W.H. Phillips, Capt. & Adjt.
   B   ..   7   ..   for O.C. 2/4 Bn. Lincs. Regt.
   C   ..   7   ..
   D   ..   7   ..
Officers Mess 4 Copies.
Q.M. T.O: M.G.O: 1 copy each.
N.C.O i/c Signallers 1 Copy.
Retained 2 copies.

WO 95/strwy/kk

12.621 43193CB00013B/2425 [2095192570]

www.ingramcontent.com/pod-product-compliance
Lightning Source LLC
Chambersburg PA
CBHW081449160426